ISBN: 9781313255387

Published by:
HardPress Publishing
8345 NW 66TH ST #2561
MIAMI FL 33166-2626

Email: info@hardpress.net
Web: http://www.hardpress.net

Profitable Pigeon Breeding

PAIR OF WHITE KINGS

PROFITABLE PIGEON BREEDING

A PRACTICAL MANUAL EXPLAINING HOW TO BREED PIGEONS SUCCESSFULLY,—WHETHER AS A HOBBY OR AS AN EXCLUSIVE BUSINESS

— BY —

F. ARTHUR HAZARD

FORMERLY MEMBER OF—
Dixie Pigeon Association.
South Carolina Poultry Breeders Association.
Board of Directors, American White King Association.
Board of Directors, American Squab Breeders Association.

FORMERLY
Secretary, American Squab Breeders Association.
President, South Carolina Pigeon Breeders Association.
1st Vice-President, American Squab Breeders Association.
Managing Owner, Hazard Squab Company, Georgetown, S. C.

AT PRESENT
Secretary, American King Club.
Member, National Pigeon Association.
Member, American Squab Breeders Association.

ILLUSTRATED

PUBLISHED BY

American Pigeon Journal Company

PUBLISHERS OF STANDARD PIGEON BOOKS

WARRENTON, MO., U. S. A.

1922

FW

Publishers' Note

We take great pleasure in presenting to the public "Profitable Pigeon Breeding," by F. Arthur Hazard, a book which will appeal particularly to the beginner. It is another one of our series of standard pigeon textbooks. Experienced breeders will find it especially valuable as a reference book and manual.

Mr. Hazard is not only a breeder of pigeons, but a recognized authority on the subject, having had a life-long experience to back up his statements. He is well known to the pigeon world as a practical writer having contributed articles for many years to the American Pigeon Journal. He knows what affects profit and loss, knows the problems of the beginner, and explains in detail the successive steps the beginner must learn in order to become a successful pigeon breeder,—whether it be merely as a hobby or as an exclusive business.

No time or expense has been spared in making this book as valuable as possible, all the illustrations being from actual photographs while the drawings were especially made by Mr. Hazard himself. The plans and specifications for the construction of pigeon houses and fly pens will prove of great value to those who contemplate building a pigeon plant or enlarging their present plant.

The book has been divided into forty chapters, thus making it not only well suited for textbook use in agricultural colleges, poultry extension courses, boys' and girls' club work, correspondence courses, but also convenient for home study.

AMERICAN PIGEON JOURNAL COMPANY.

F. ARTHUR HAZARD

FOREWORD

Years ago when the writer was but a small boy, my father owned and bred English Pouters and Fantail Pigeons. Not only was he fond of them, but I was proud of them. The loft in which these birds were kept has long since been torn down but the memory of it still lingers in my mind. It was then that my love for pigeons was kindled, only to grow stronger and deeper as the years have passed. These years have brought wider experiences to me, and by these hard earned experiences have I been able to present this book to you in its present form.

Though I first knew the Fancy breeds my work with pigeons has drifted to the Utility, yet I admire practically every one of the Fancy breeds. Having had long experience with the utility breeds and feeling that there is need for another work on the subject of pigeon breeding I have been prompted to write this book. No man knows all about this subject and I sincerely trust that in reading these chapters you will not feel that I have placed my knowledge above that of all other writers. I have only endeavored to present the subject as carefully and concisely as possible and I earnestly hope that what is contained herein will accomplish the purpose for which it was intended, namely: a textbook for the novice and a hand book for the experienced breeder. This being done I will feel greatly rewarded for my work, for the writing of this book has been a pleasure indeed.

In the breed articles the author has tried to be fair and not set any one breed upon a pinnacle and praise it while trampling down the others. Each breed has its faults as well as its good qualities. I have tried to show both as I see them. If any one breed were vastly superior to all others I am inclined to think we would all want to keep that breed, but difference of opinion, holding sway as it always does, makes us differ and gives each breed a chance.

The last part of the book has been given over to the

publication of descriptive standards and illustrations of several of the more prominent of the Fancy breeds. This has been primarily to show off these grand birds and to endeavor to interest more breeders in keeping a few fancy birds. The more good fellowship we can create between the lovers of the utility and of the fancy the greater is our chance, and at least the hope of the writer, to bring more birds to our leading shows and make these shows wider in scope and not merely have them favoring, for the greater part, either the fancy or the utility.

To those who have so kindly given us the pictures used in making the illustrations in this book, I wish to express my sincerest thanks. May I not mention the names of the following:

Eugene Altpeter, Milwaukee, Wis.
H. W. Barnett, Oakland, Calif.
H. B. Behrens, Philadelphia, Pa.
Alan G. Curry, Hayward, Calif.
Fairview Pigeon Lofts, Trenton, N. J.
J. W. Geddes, Egg Harbor City, N. J.
A. J. Gies, Schenectady, N. Y.
W. T. Helm, El Rio, Oxnard, Calif.
Frank H. Hollman, Warrenton, Mo.
C. R. King, Hayward, Calif.
Edwin W. Knowles, Baltimore, Md.
O. B. Lindberg, Los Angeles, Cal.
Longwood Squab Farm, Longwood, Fla.
Marion Martin, El Paso, Texas.
James R. S. May, Knoxville, Tenn.
B. A. Mitchell, Orenco, Ore.
D. J. Ogilive, Oceanside, L. I., N. Y.
Oscar W. Opsann, New Rochelle, N. Y.
Jack M. Pun, Stockton, Calif.
Ned Reed, Puxico, Mo.
F. A. Rommell, Baltimore, Md.
Rosenthal Bros., St. Louis, Mo.
Edgar Satterthwaite, Stanton, Del.
L. N. Smith, Minneapolis, Minn.
E. H. Trissler, Lancaster, Pa.
Harry C. Weber, Hagerstown, Md.
Paul Weyer, Elmhurst, Calif.
Whelan & Son, Kansas City, Mo.
Wilson Pigeon Farm, Wilson, Kan.

It is indeed gratifying to know the true spirit of co-operation that exists among the pigeon breeders of this country and great credit is due to those who went to so much trouble to assist the author for they have manifested a spirit, which if it is shown in other branches of our fraternity, is bound to bring the pigeon industry up to a higher plane and make it even more attractive to the novice.

F. ARTHUR HAZARD.

Augusta, Georgia.
August 1, 1922.

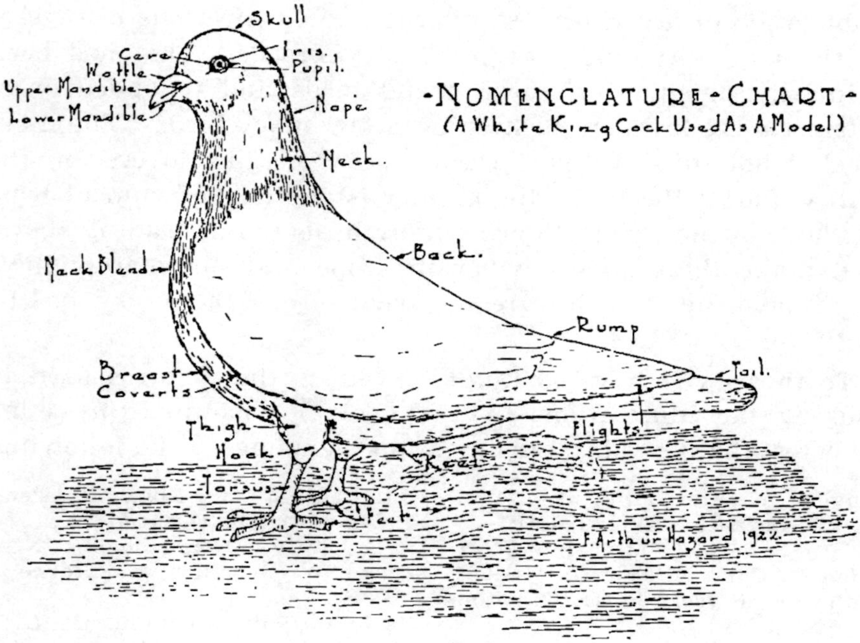

·NOMENCLATURE·CHART·
(A White King Cock Used As A Model.)

Glossary of Breeding Terms

BEAK—The combination of the upper and lower mandible.

BREED—A distinct race of pigeons.

BREEDER—A person who breeds pigeons.

CERE—The fleshy circle around a pigeon's eye.

COVERTS—The lesser or short feathers covering the upper portion of the primaries and secondaries of the wing.

COW-HOCKS—Legs bent too much at knees.

DOWN FACE—The face pulled down and back so as to place the beak almost against upper throat feathers.

FLIGHTS—Principal feathers of wing or those on outside edge, otherwise known as primaries.

HOG BACK—Round shouldered.

KEEL—The continuation of the breast bone under body of bird.

KNOCK KNEED—Knees bent inwards toward each other.

MANDIBLE—One half of beak, the beak being made up of upper and lower mandibles.

PINCHED BACK—Small narrow back.

PINCHED HEAD—Narrow head.

PRIMARIES—See flights.

ROACH BACK—Hump on back.

RUMP—That portion of back immediately over vent.

SECONDARIES—The lesser of the longest wing feathers or those nearest the body when wing is slightly outstretched.

SPLIT TAIL—Tail feathers separated, a part being carried to either side.

STANDARD BRED—Pigeons that are bred to a recognized standard.

SMUT—Dark, slaty colored feathers in undercolor.

SQUAB—A young pigeon that has not reached its fifth week of age.

UNDER COLOR—The color of feathers just under the surface of the Plumage.

WATTLE—The fleshy substance on the beak of a pigeon.

WING BUTT—The front curved portion of wing when folded.

TABLE OF CONTENTS

CHAPTER V

CHAPTER VI

CHAPTER VII

CHAPTER VIII

CHAPTER IX

CHAPTER X

CHAPTER XI

CHAPTER XX

CHAPTER XXI

CHAPTER XXII

CHAPTER XXIII

CHAPTER XXIV

CHAPTER XXV

CHAPTER XXVI

CHAPTER XXVII

CHAPTER XXVIII

CHAPTER XXIX

CHAPTER XXX

CHAPTER XXXI

CHAPTER XXXII

PROFITABLE PIGEON BREEDING

CHAPTER I

THE START

Advice to the Novice—Fitting up a Temporary Home for the Birds—Needed Accessories.

It has been said, and rightly so, that every man should have a hobby. The average man is a hard working individual who is constantly interested in his business and little does he realize that "All work and no play makes Jack a dull boy." It therefore behooves us all to have a hobby of some sort. Those who love bird life can find unlimited pleasure in the breeding of pigeons and besides, as they become more proficient in the art of breeding and caring for them, they can have a nice little income from their birds.

Too much has been written about the enormous profits to be realized from squab plants. Unscrupulous men have painted glaring pictures of such profits merely to sell the beginner a few pairs of birds. This is wrong and it is to the interest of the pigeon fraternity to discourage such schemes. The writer has proven to his own satisfaction that money can be made from selling squabs to the markets, in producing and selling breeding stock and exhibition specimens, but he is not the kind to lead any beginner into believing that the squab or pigeon business is a get-rich-quick scheme. Some of the breeders in the past have issued literature that has been so worded as to make the beginner believe that all he had to do was to buy a few pairs of birds, place them in any kind of an outbuilding and give them feed and water every day and his fortune would soon come to him. In order to make money out of the squab business one must apply sound business methods to it. Lack of system and poor business judgment will be conducive only of ruin as in any other line of endeavor.

In making a start we wish to advise all beginners to act wisely in the purchase of their foundation stock no matter what the breed might be nor what the variety. Do not try to get something for nothing for a case of this kind is usually the forerunner of bitter disappointment if not of complete failure. Decide upon what breed you wish to make a start with and then purchase a few pairs of high grade birds from a reliable breeder. Do not purchase your foundation stock from any individual or concern printing wonderful stories about their extra grade stock. The honest and reliable breeder does not have to print such stories in order to dispose of his birds. Be careful not to buy from a dealer but rather from a breeder who raises all the birds he offers for sale. It he be honest he will, no doubt, be willing to give you a liberal guarantee. Do not purchase many birds at the start but be content with a few. It is far more to your advantage to purchase three pairs of birds at five dollars per pair than fifteen pairs at one dollar per pair even though the amount invested is the same. Good breeding stock, like good machinery, cannot be purchased cheaply. Remember that you are laying a foundation upon which a future is to be built and the more solid the foundation the more secure the future will be. No wise manufacturer will equip his factory with old worn-out machinery because he realizes that he cannot produce efficiently with such equipment. So with a squab plant, the pigeons are the machinery.

You have a right to get what you pay for and it is to your interest to insist on getting sound healthy breeding birds. The birds with which you make your start should be not less than one year old and not more than three years of age. These birds should come to you properly mated and banded so that you can distinguish the mated pairs by looking at the leg bands.

A pretentious home is not needed for breeding squabs. Any

outhouse that can be made damp proof and wind proof will serve the purpose in a very satisfactory manner for a while. The floor of this house should be lifted off the ground at least one foot and should be so constructed as to permit a free circulation of air beneath the floor at all times. All cracks in the walls and roof should be stopped up so as to keep out the wind and rain. This can be easily done by covering sides and roof of the house with a medium grade of roofing paper. A window should be provided so that the birds may get out into the fly pen. This fly pen, which will be hereafter called the fly, is nothing more or less than a large wire cage with a frame work of two inch by four inch timbers covered with one or two inch mesh poultry wire. The fly that has proven most satisfactory to the writer is one ten feet long, eight feet wide and six feet six inches tall, though, owing to the different designs of pigeon houses they sometimes have to be made a trifle higher and wider but we would recommend that the fly never be made over eight feet high as the builder will waste material and will always be at a disadvantage in that he will have a hard time catching his birds when he wants to do so. Around the sides of this fly is placed a one inch by six inch board known as a running board. This board is set out about six inches from the wire so that when the birds turn around on it they will not break their tail feathers in the wire. It serves as a place where the birds can sun themselves and rest when off duty.

In the fly we should provide some kind of receptacle for watering the birds. If running water is not to be used a one gallon drinking fountain should be placed in each pen or fly. These can be bought at almost any seed store or poultry supply house.

A bath pan should also be provided, for pigeons are extremely fond of bathing in water and it is very beneficial to them. A large dishpan is just the very thing for this purpose and cheap ones may be had at the ten cent stores.

In the house or loft we should provide nests. For the beginner these can be orange crates, laid on their sides, in tiers.

Each crate should have a three inch strip nailed across the front at the bottom. This strip is needed to keep the nesting material in place and to also keep the squabs from falling out of the nests. Two nests or one crate should be provided for each pair of birds to be kept. A few extra nests will not be out of place in the loft.

A lump of rock salt, such as is put in horses' mangers, should be placed on the ground of the fly. Pigeons need salt just as do human beings and it should be fed to them in this manner. Never, under any conditions, feed loose table salt as the birds will eat too much of it at one time and die as a result. They will peck at the rock salt from time to time and derive a great deal of benefit from it.

In the squab house should be placed a crate of some kind preferably a strawberry crate. In this is kept hay, straw, tobacco stems or pine needles. These are the materials which are most commonly used by pigeons in building their nests. This material should be on hand at all times.

A feed box of some kind should be provided and the birds fed only from this box. Never throw grain on the ground. Several different types of feeders are shown elsewhere on the pages of this book and the beginner should have one of them made for his use rather than take any chances in feeding in other ways.

Having gotten everything in readiness and the birds in their new quarters go into the loft and remain quietly for a few minutes each day. The birds at first will fly about in excitement but as they begin to know you they will take your visits as a matter of fact and not be afraid of you. Tame them as much as possible for it means contentment among them and contented birds breed much better.

Elsewhere on the pages of this book are shown plans for better squab houses and their accessories and as your plant grows you can erect buildings of this better type. They will prove to be labor savers in every way.

CHAPTER II

SELECTING THE BREED

The Leading Commercial Squab Producing Pigeons—Advice Against Using the Common Pigeon.

Which breed shall I select? This is a question that we are confident has puzzled many a beginner. To the mind of the writer it seems to be a question which should be solved by the one asking it, after he or she has fully looked into the facts concerning the different breeds. In order to assist the novice we have, therefore, prepared chapters covering the different squab producing varieties. These should be of great value in helping the beginner make a wise selection.

The writer considers the following to be the best breeds for commercial squab production. The White King, the Silver King, the Homer, the Carneau, the Runt, the Mondaine, the Maltese and the Hungarian. Of all of these the Kings, Homer and Carneau are probably the most prolific, taken as a breed and the most profitable. However, the others are excellent squab producers and all can be relied upon if properly handled. The Homer is one of the most used breeds for this purpose, probably the most widely used, but the other breeds are rapidly coming to their own and today we find large commercial squab plants where there are but few Homers.

Our advice to the novice is to breed a thoroughbred bird, never a crossbred or mongrel and never waste good blood lines of two different breeds by mating them together to get a crossbred squab. Under no circumstances should one breed the mongrel or common pigeon. The latter will not produce as many nor as large squabs as thoroughbred specimens.

Having selected a breed stick to it and strive to get the best there is out of that breed. Select a breed that will produce squabs weighing around a pound each when dressed, a breed that will throw white meated squabs and a large number of them. Any of the breeds we have mentioned above will prove profitable provided the proper breeding is behind them.

It is not an unwise plan for the novice to visit several different squab breeders who have high grade stock and see for himself just what the birds are before purchasing.

CHAPTER III

LAYING AND HATCHING

The Cock Drives the Hen—One Egg Hatches Before the Other—Changing Squabs from One Nest to Another—The Growth of Squabs—Squabs fed by Parents—The Most Profitable Birds to Own.

In your visits to a pigeon loft you will notice a pair of birds billing and kissing. This is the natural forerunner of breeding. The cock bird will soon be seen to tread. Then he "drives" the hen, following her around from perch to perch, on to the running boards, on to the ground and so on until he finally succeeds in getting her into the nest which they have selected. He will keep right in behind her and peck at her until she obeys

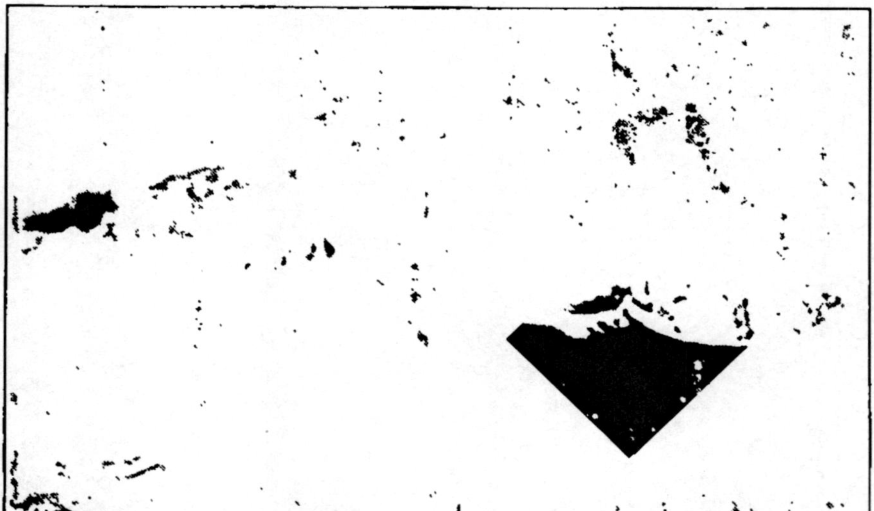

SQUABS ONE DAY OLD AND THREE DAYS OLD
Photo from Longwood Squab Farm, Longwood, Fla.

his desire for her to go to their nest. The cock will be heard to make a cooing sound to her and presently they start carrying nesting material up to the nest piece by piece until the nest is completed. The cock is most usually the one that carries the nesting material. The hen then lays an egg and skips a day before she lays another. Pigeons lay only two eggs before they begin to set on them or incubate them. From the time she lays the first egg both cock and hen share in incubating the

CARNEAU SQUABS AT THREE WEEKS AND FOUR WEEKS OF AGE WHEN THEY ARE READY FOR MARKET
Photo from Longwood Squab Farm, Longwood, Fla.

eggs, the cock going on duty about ten o'clock in the morning and remaining on the eggs until about four o'clock in the afternoon. The hen then goes on the nest and covers the eggs until the next morning at ten o'clock. They alternate in this manner for a period of seventeen days, at the expiration of which time the eggs will hatch, one egg invariably hatching before the other one. For this reason one squab is almost always a little larger than the other, and of course the first one to hatch has the advantage in getting food first. It is not a bad idea, therefore, where squabs are to be killed later, to change them from one nest to another so that both squabs in any nest will be of the same size and have the same chance at getting food. Where one squab is larger than the other the larger one usually gets the most food and very naturally grows faster and larger. The writer does not advocate this change in a case where the squabs are bred from exhibition specimens and are, themselves, to be saved for it is not at all unlikely that a mistake may occur in the record keeping, thus losing track of the parentage of the squabs.

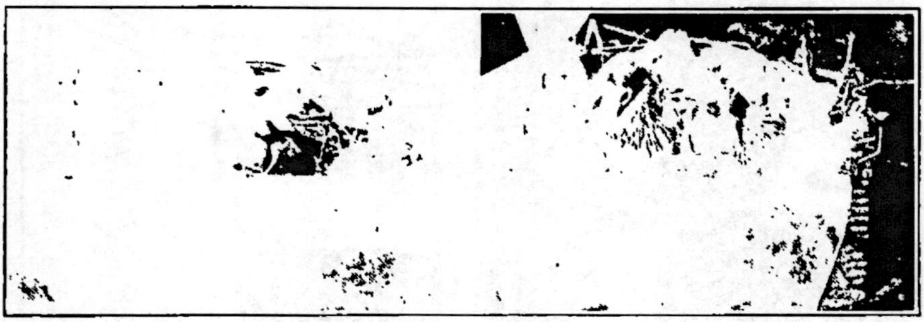

WHITE KING SQUABS THREE DAYS OLD AND TWELVE DAYS OLD
Photo from Jack M. Pun, Stockton, Calif.

When squabs are born they look like little yellow balls of down. At the end of the first week of their lives they still have this suit but have about trebled their former size. The expiration of two weeks finds them very much larger and practically covered with feathers. At three weeks old they are almost completely covered with all of their feathers and at four weeks of age they are entirely feathered and ready to leave the nest and go to market or to the floor of the loft if they are to be saved for breeding purposes. They are allowed to remain in the lofts about one week after leaving the nests, if they are to be saved. This is done to give them a chance to learn, from the older birds, how to eat from the feed box and drink from the watering fountain.

While the parents are incubating the eggs a milky white substance forms in their crops which is known as "Pigeon's Milk." This substance is the first food a squab receives. The squab sticks its beak into the beak of the parent bird and he or she, as the case may be, with a muscular action, forces this milk into the throat of the squab. For the first five days of the squab's life it is fed on this milk. After that time this milk gradually grows thicker and thicker and begins to contain more

WHITE KING SQUABS EIGHTEEN DAYS OLD AND FOUR WEEKS OLD.

Photo from Jack M. Fun, Stockton, Calif.

and more whole grain until the squab is about ten days old when it starts getting whole grain and water from the crops of the parent birds.

During the time that the birds have squabs in the nests they will, at feeding time, eat as much as possible and then drink all the water they can. Then they fly off to their nest and stuff the squabs with this mixture.

A good pair of breeding birds, and the most profitable ones to own, are those that will, when a pair of squabs have reached two weeks of age, get busy again and start another nest nearby. The same action as described above goes on again. As soon as the hen lays her second set of eggs the cock bird takes almost complete charge of the first squabs, attending to them when off the second eggs, rearing them until they are weaned at between four and five weeks of age. Birds of this kind are often referred to as "Double Nest Workers" and are, as I have said, the most profitable ones to own.

CARNEAU SQUAB ABOUT THREE WEEKS OLD

CHAPTER IV

FEEDING

Special Attention to Feeding—Grains Eaten by Pigeons—Feeding Qualities of the Various Grains—Advice to the Beginner to Buy Manufactured Feeds—Names of Leading Brands of Pigeon Feeds. —Analysis of Feedstuffs—Table Showing Composition of Feedstuffs—Three Feed Formulae with Description Showing How they Are Worked Out—Changing Fats to Nitrogen Free Extracts—Health Grits—Health Grit Formula.

Pigeons, in confinement, require special attention as regards their feed. In their wild state they select and consume a great variety of grain. They are not carnivorous or flesh eating birds but live only by eating grain and green foods. Therefore, we must provide them with this same variety of grain when we confine them. Many novices in breeding pigeons have failed solely because they did not know the necessity of properly feeding their birds. One thing to be remembered above all others is that pigeons, like poultry, must be given a balanced ration for without this they will only live and cannot produce plump squabs nor many of them because they are not receiving that which goes toward making eggs, etc.

The grains used in feeding pigeons are whole corn, Canada peas, cow peas, mixed field peas, wheat, rice, millet, kafir corn, hemp, buckwheat, sunflower seed, peanuts, milo maize, feterita, etc. However, none of these grains should be fed by itself for any length of time for that grain, no matter which one we may select, it will not contain the correct amount of the constituents which go toward making a balanced ration and therefore is by itself not a balanced ration. Moreover, as stated before, pigeons need a variety of grain. These are the two principal reasons why we feed mixed grains to our birds in confinement.

Besides grain pigeons require green food in some form and it should be fed as often as possible and the breeder should try to vary this form of food. We use Swiss chard, lettuce leaves, cabbage leaves, sprouted oats and green bean vines. It is to the advantage of the breeder to have a small piece of ground where he can grow one or two of the above mentioned green foods as in doing this he will get them cheaply and will have them on hand more or less all of the time. In feeding sprouted oats never, under any conditions, feed the sprouted seed but only the green blades. Pigeons are especially fond of greens and will rush for them when put into the flys.

One will find bread crumbs an excellent food for pigeons and something that they always devour eagerly. Stale bread is usually obtainable at bakeries at a most reasonable price and its use will help materially to cut down the feed bills. The baker, as a rule, is anxious to get rid of such bread at a nominal price. Never use it, however, should it show any signs of being mouldy. The writer admits that he does not know what good the birds derive from eating bread crumbs but it has always seemed to do them absolutely no harm and in that it helps to reduce the feed bills we recommend its use.

There is on the market today what is known as Wild Grass Seed Mixture. It is usually made up of various wild grass seeds and is a most excellent feed for pigeons. This feed seems to supply a great many seeds which pigeons would get were they flying at large but which are rarely, if ever, placed in commercial pigeon feeds. This mixture is very reasonable in price and should be used freely as it is relished very much by the birds. It seems to tone them up.

We will take several grains that we have mentioned above and see just wherein they are or are not good for pigeons.

Cracked corn is very deceptive and I am sincere in my belief that it should never be fed under any circumstances. I am also firm in my belief that cracked corn is the cause of more canker than any other thing. It will absorb moisture and become mouldy in a very short time and mouldy feed invariably leads to one of two things—canker or roup. Use only sound, hard corn and best of all Argentine Flint corn. This is a small yellow grain that is very hard.

In passing from cracked corn we will consider what is known as Scratch Feed, such as is fed to poultry. Do not resort to this feed if it can possibly be avoided. It is usually priced at a much lower figure than mixed pigeon feed and in order to economize the novice will, in a great many cases, use it and think that he is acting judiciously. This mixture was never intended for pigeons and does not carry the correct amount of nutriment nor usually the proper grains. The scratch feed is invariably mixed with cracked corn and it is, therefore, I consider, dangerous to feed. It may well be used for a while but our experience has been that feeding it is taking a great chance.

Wheat is a splendid feed but, in a way, it is also a dangerous one. The danger in feeding wheat lies in the fact that feeding too much of it is very weakening to the birds. Birds fed an excessive amount of it become unable to fly. New soft white wheat should never be used. Feed only hard red winter wheat. This grain is relished very much by pigeons.

Canada peas make an excellent pigeon feed. They are the cleanest and best of all peas for pigeons and if possible to get them at a reasonable price they should be fed freely. If one is unable to get them for any reason cow peas or mixed field peas may be substituted, in fact either of these make an excellent feed. The Canada peas, however, contain 23.7% protein as against 22.4% for mixed peas and 23.5% for cow peas. Therefore the Canada peas should be given the preference when the prices for the three are equal.

Rice is a necessary feed once in a while. This grain is used principally to check loose bowels but it will constipate the birds if fed too often. The writer makes it a practice to feed his birds once a week with rice, using only a small amount at a time and feeds it separately from the regular ration.

Golden millet is relished very much. This grain is low in protein but it seems to be excellent for a change in diet and should be fed once or twice a week in small amounts.

Kafir corn is a splendid feed and can be used freely. It is invariably lower in price than most other grains.

Hemp seed is very fattening. It is probably liked more by pigeons than any other grain. On account of its usual high cost it can only be fed very sparingly, but the breeder will find this grain of much value. It is a fine conditioner and in getting birds ready for the show room we feed it rather liberally as it puts them in the pink of condition in a short time. Besides what hemp there might be in the mixed feed we advise feeding it separately, in small amounts, once a week. The same thing might be said of sunflower seed.

Peanuts, of late years, have become quite widely used for pigeon feed due to the fact that they contain a very large percentage of protein, it being 27.9% or more than that contained in any other grain or food which we give to pigeons with the exception of the soy bean and this is not fed very often. They have come into such general use because of their lower cost than peas for which grain they form a substitute. It is best to feed the small Spanish peanuts or the cracked ones.

Before going further into the details of feeding, a word of advice to the novice may be of some help. There are on the market several well known brands of pigeon feed and we would surely advise the beginner to use one or more of them until he or she thoroughly learns feeds and understands food values. Later he can work out his own balanced ration formulae and mix the feed at his own plant. We give here a list of high grade ready mixed feeds:

BRAND	MANUFACTURER	ADDRESS
Cornell	Blamberg Brothers	Baltimore, Md.
Oriole	Wm. G. Scarlett & Co.	Baltimore, Md.
Shawnee	Wood, Stubbs & Co.	Louisville, Ky.
Red Wing	Wood, Stubbs & Co.	Louisville, Ky.
Challenge	Wood, Stubbs & Co.	Louisville, Ky.
Purina Pigeon Chow	Ralston Purina Co.	St. Louis, Mo.
Hollybrook	T. W. Wood & Son	Richmond, Va.
Famabella	Caughey-Jossman Co.	Detroit, Mich.

The writer has used all of the above brands and can heartily recommend each of them for they are all balanced rations.

In making a study of grains for pigeon feed we find five constituents that enter into their composition and these must be so proportioned as to form a properly balanced ration. They are: water, ash, protein, carbohydrates and fat. Carbohydrates in turn are divided into two subheads, i. e., fiber and nitrogen free extracts.

Water is contained in all feeds to a certain extent. In looking over the accompanying table showing the composition of pigeon foodstuffs we find that the water contained in the different grains varies from 7.5% to 15%.

Ash consists of mineral matter including lime, soda, iron, potash, etc.

Protein is that constituent which builds up the body in that it manufactures flesh, feathers, blood, muscle, eggs, etc. It is the most important of the constituents entering into the make-up of pigeon feeds. Without the proper amount of it we cannot expect to get eggs nor can we expect any but scrawny squabs that may or may not live after birth. To keep pigeons in proper condition to work efficiently it is necessary to feed the proper amount of protein because it is that substance which has to be relied upon to repair the body in most of its parts and keep it in first class working order. But, on the other hand, it is dangerous to feed an excessive amount of protein because, fed in this manner, it proves to be injurious to the internal organs of the bird. Scientific investigation and careful study has shown us that the percentage of protein that should be used is from fourteen to fifteen which means that the protein content of every one hundred pounds of pigeon feed should be from fourteen to fifteen per cent of protein or that many pounds of it.

Carbohydrates or nitrogen-free extracts consist of sugars and starches and it is this material which supplies the heat and energy to the bird's body. In referring to our table showing the composition of pigeon foodstuffs we find a greater percentage of this constituent in the grains than any of the others.

Fats likewise furnish heat and energy for the body and are very important. Too much fat, however, is dangerous as it will cause internal trouble.

Fiber is usually composed of the shell or husks of the grain and is invariably very indigestible. We find that the grains which we feed to pigeons have, as a rule, a very low percentage of fiber and we, therefore, take but very little consideration of it in making up our feed formulae.

Thus we see that every constituent has its part to play in the composition of feeds and it is by the proper proportioning of them that we get a balanced ration or a ration which is composed of such feeds in such proportions to furnish the necessary and correct amount of nutrients.

COMPOSITION OF PIGEON FEEDSTUFFS

(As compiled by the United States Department of Agriculture.)

Feedstuffs	Water	Ash	Protein	Carbohydrates Fiber	Carbohydrates Nitrogen-free extracts	Fat
Corn	10.9	1.5	10.5	2.1	69.6	5.4
Wheat	10.5	1.8	11.9	1.8	71.9	2.1
Kafir Corn	12.8	2.1	9.1	2.6	69.8	3.6
Oats	11.0	3.0	11.8	9.5	59.7	5.0
Canada Peas	15.0	2.4	23.7	7.9	50.2	.8
Peas	13.4	2.4	22.4	6.4	52.6	3.0
Cowpeas	11.9	3.4	23.5	3.8	55.7	1.7
Peanuts	7.5	2.4	27.9	7.0	15.6	39.6
Buckwheat	12.6	2.0	10.0	8.7	64.5	2.2
Egyptian Corn	12.6	1.9	9.9	1.9	69.7	3.9
Millet	12.1	2.8	10.9	8.1	62.6	3.5
Hempseed	8.0	2.0	10.0	14.0	45.0	21.0
Sunflower Seed	8.6	2.6	15.3	29.9	21.4	21.2
Maize	12.0	1.4	11.0	3.0	69.7	2.3
Feterita	11.5	1.3	13.0	2.0	67.4	2.7
Soy Beans	7.7	5.7	35.4	4.6	21.6	20.3

Having the above before us we can figure out numerous feed formulae, any one of which will prove a good one and which will aid us in providing a variety of feeds.

I have here worked out three formulae:

NUMBER ONE:

	Protein	Fiber	Fat	Carbo'ts	Ash	Water
Peas 30 lbs...	7.11	2.37	.24	15.06	.72	.45
Corn 30 lbs....	3.15	.63	1.62	20.88	.45	3.27
Kafir 30 lbs....	2.73	.78	1.08	20.94	.53	3.84
Wheat 10 lbs....	1.19	.54	.21	7.19	.18	1.05
100 lbs....	14.18	4.32	3.15	64.07	1.98	12.61

In referring to the first table we see that 100 pounds of Canada peas contain 23.7% of protein. In our formula above we have used thirty pounds or three-tenths of a hundred pounds therefore we multiply 23.7 by .3 and get 7.11. Likewise, we see that 100 pounds of Canada peas contain 7.9% of fiber. Therefore we multiply 7.9 by .3 and get 2.37% or the amount of fiber contained in thirty pounds of this grain. By this method of referring to the table on each constituent and multiplying the percentage per 100 pounds by the fractional part of 100 pounds we find the percentage of that constituent for the amount of grain used. The formula just worked out is a good one in that it contains the correct amount of protein, it is low in fiber and has a moderate amount of fat.

NUMBER TWO:

	Protein	Fiber	Fat	Carbo'ts	Ash	Water
Can. Peas 30 lbs.	7.11	2.37	.24	15.06	.72	.45
Corn 25 lbs.	2.63	.53	1.35	17.40	.38	2.73
Kafir 25 lbs.	2.27	.65	.90	17.45	.53	3.20
Wheat 20 lbs.	2.38	1.08	.42	14.38	.36	2.10
100 lbs.	14.39	4.63	2.91	64.29	1.98	8.48

NUMBER THREE:

	Protein	Fiber	Fat	Carbo'ts	Ash	Water
Kafir 30 lbs..	2.73	.78	1.08	20.94	.63	3.84
Corn 20 lbs..	2.10	.42	1.08	13.92	.30	2.18
Peanuts 30 lbs..	8.37	2.10	1.19	4.68	.72	2.25
Wheat 10 lbs..	1.19	.54	.21	7.19	.18	1.05
Hemp 5 lbs..	.50	.70	1.05	2.25	.10	1.05
Millet 5 lbs..	.55	.41	.18	3.13	.14	.61
100 lbs.	15.44	4.95	4.79	52.11	2.07	10.98

Thus we see that we can go on and on making up different feed formulae but we have another important factor that we must take into consideration and that factor is the nutritive ratio of feeds. This ratio is the proportion of the protein to the total nitrogen-free extract. We first find out how much protein our formula shows and it should be around 14% to 15%. Having this we calculate the total percentage of the constituents. Next we change the fat into nitrogen-free extract by multiplying the fat by 2¼ and adding the result to the nitrogen-free extract. This total should be from four and one-half to five times the total amount of protein to have a correct nutritive ratio. Thus we see that my first two formulac are all right and the last one, while it carries the correct amount of protein and will prove to be a good feeding formula, it is just a little shy in the nutritive ratio.

The breeder can easily work out various formulae from the above information that will provide his birds with balanced rations and a wide variety of feeds.

Inasmuch as pigeons have no teeth we must provide them with some sort of material which will grind their food in the crop. This is taken care of by the use of health grit. This grit is a composition of clean sharp sand, small shells, charcoal, salt and some mineral matter, together with a tonic. It is extremely essential to birds in confinement and should always be in the lofts. The health grits that are most highly recommended and those that we have used, are:

BRAND	MANUFACTURER	ADDRESS
Red Cross	J. W. Williamson Co.	Glassboro, N. J.
Fousts	George Foust Co.	Guilford, Conn.

The following is a formula given to the writer several years ago and which makes an excellent health grit mixture.

Sifted Sand, 80 pounds; Venetian Red, 8 ounces; Gentian Root, 6 ounces; Powdered Alum, 4 ounces; Table Salt, 6.5 pounds; Oyster Shells (Chick size), 9 pounds; Charcoal, 3 pounds.

In making up this mixture add just a little water while mixing it.

In addition to the health grit that is fed we would advise a small container of charcoal in each loft as the charcoal can do the birds no harm and is an excellent regulator.

In concluding this chapter I would advise any breeder to order his grain with care. Be sure from whom you buy because it is absolutely essential to your success to feed nothing but hard, sound, sweet grain. Do not lay in too large a supply at one time unless you have the proper facilities for storing it. I trust that this chapter will help many to overcome one of the most difficult problems of feeding pigeons namely, a change of diet and providing balanced rations.

CHAPTER V

HOUSING

No Need of Ornamental Lofts—Description of Materials to be Used—Fly Pens—The Open Front House—Bill of Material for the Open Front House—Two Pen Pigeon House and Fly, with Bill of Material—Three Pen Pigeon House with Bill of Material—Individual Runt Breeding Pen with Bill of Material—Monitor Type Squab House with Bill of Material—The Squab Dressing Plant with Bill of Material—Layout of a Plant to Accommodate 1000 Pairs of Pigeons.

In the first chapter of this book I made the assertion that a pretentious home is not necessary for breeding squabs. This is very true and while a more or less ordinary loft will do for a while, the breeder should strive to house his birds in better homes; ones which are so designed as to be sanitary, comforta-

SQUAB BREEDING PENS
Photo from Jack M. Pun, Stockton, Calif.

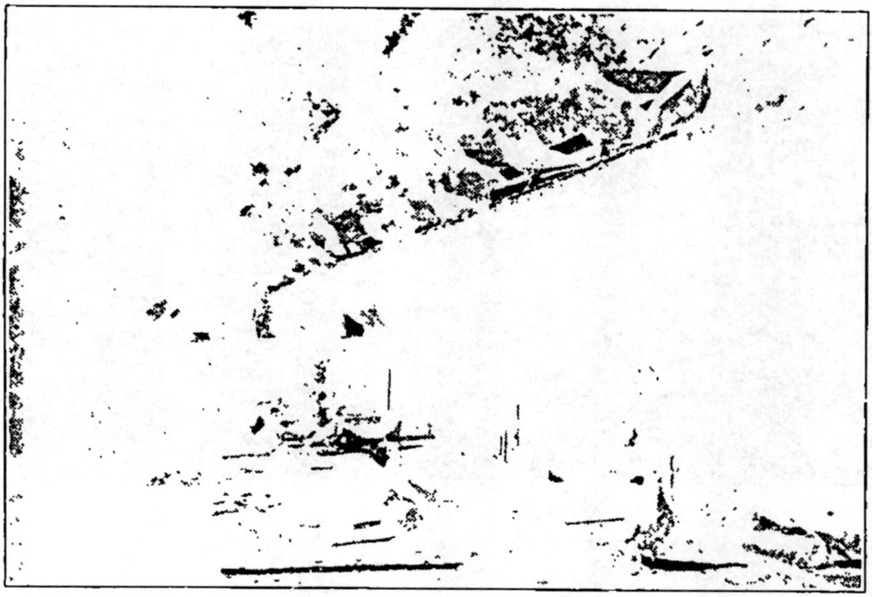

LOOKING THROUGH SQUAB BREEDING PENS
Note Open Front House, Low Flys and absence of Ladders.—Photo from Jack M. Pun, Stockton, Calif.

ble and economical as well as labor saving. Aside from this, as the plant grows it should be built with some definite style of construction in view so that the whole will at least be pleasing to the eye, not only of the owner, but of the visitor as well. Visitors cannot become favorably impressed with a general mixup of different styles of lofts. Having had considerable experience in designing pigeon lofts of various types and styles we have deemed it very wise to go into this subject of housing very carefully and have endeavored to present to our readers some definite clear-cut working drawings of different houses which we believe will prove beneficial in many ways. Another thing that has prompted me to be so careful with this chapter and cover the subject so thoroughlty is the fact that since I first made some drawings for the American Pigeon Journal several years ago I frequently get requests for help along this line. Owing to lack of space I cannot go into minute detail

ANOTHER VIEW OF OPEN FRONT HOUSE
Photo from Jack M. Pun, Stockton, Calif.

ONE OF THE LARGEST PIGEON PLANTS IN THE WORLD
Photo from King Lofts, Hayward, Calif.

with the drawings but I do feel that enough has been shown on my plates so that even an ordinary "jack-leg" can work by them. However, should the readers of this book fail to understand any drawing the writer will be pleased to explain any point by letter.

It has been my idea to design these lofts shown herewith with sensible economy in mind. There is positively no need of building ornamental lofts for pigeons such as a great many of you have seen pictures of. That type of house is rapidly passing out of existence and rightly so. What is needed as an abode for pigeons is a substantial, well ventilated, well arranged loft of plain lines. Drafts must be kept out, dampness must be eliminated, light and plenty of fresh air must be admitted, nests must be arranged to be readily accessible for the birds yet

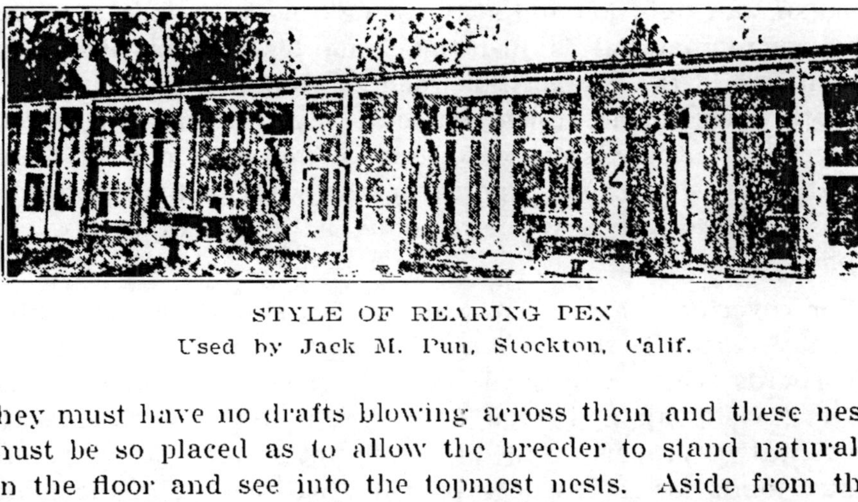

STYLE OF REARING PEN
Used by Jack M. Pun, Stockton, Calif.

they must have no drafts blowing across them and these nests must be so placed as to allow the breeder to stand naturally on the floor and see into the topmost nests. Aside from this the building must be substantially built so as to last. These things have all been taken into consideration and if one follows the plans as I have shown them I do not think that he will go very far wrong.

There is one thing which will be plainly noticed about my drawings and the following plan descriptions and that is, I have not mentioned what wood to use. My advice is to use that wood which is cheapest in your particular community. Here in the South we very naturally use pine because it is very plentiful and therefore the cheapest.

In some cases I have shown shiplap used as flooring. This will work nicely but a rough board floor will answer the purpose just as well provided the board edges are square and straight and the boards are nailed up hard against each other so as to keep out dampness from below. Of course tongued and grooved flooring blind-nailed would make a much smoother and tighter flooring but it is far too expensive. Therefore we must resort to something cheaper. In my native city there is manufactured what is known as "cull roofers" which are tongued and grooved boards that have been dressed and are used for sheathing on cheap work. We have used this most successfully for squab house floors and find that it makes a good smooth tight job and at the same time an inexpensive one. This same material is just the thing for roof sheathing on which is laid the composition roofing. It is necessary to have smooth even surface upon which to lay this kind of roofing material or otherwise it will become uneven and hold water and this is what is not wanted at all. Composition roofing is nothing more or less than a roofing built up out of tar, felt, asphalt, etc.

For covering the exterior walls I find shiplap a good thing and my reason is this, it makes a good vertical joint between the boards which will shed water in a good strong rain and is very easily applied. Not only this, it makes a tight draft-proof wall if properly nailed. Never put shiplap on with horizontal joints for if you do rain water will collect in the joints and rot the boards. Square-edge boards may be used and put on with vertical joints and these joints may be stripped or covered with a one-inch by three-inch strip. However putting these strips on requires more labor, more nails and more lumber so it seems as if the advantage is in favor of the shiplap. If one wishes to do so he may use beveled siding, $\frac{5}{8}$ in. x $5\frac{1}{2}$ in. showing $4\frac{1}{2}$ in. to the weather. This will make a neat job yet it will not make as tight and durable a job as the shiplap. To my mind the shiplap is the very best thing that can be used for this purpose.

I have shown 2 in. by 4 in. studs throughout in my drawings though I have known some breeders to use 2 in. by 3 in. I do not think the latter strong enough though of course they can be used. The studs in all of the buildings shown in this chapter have been placed in the most economical manner I believe.

Either brick piers or wooden posts may be used as a foundation upon which to build the houses or if one wishes to do so

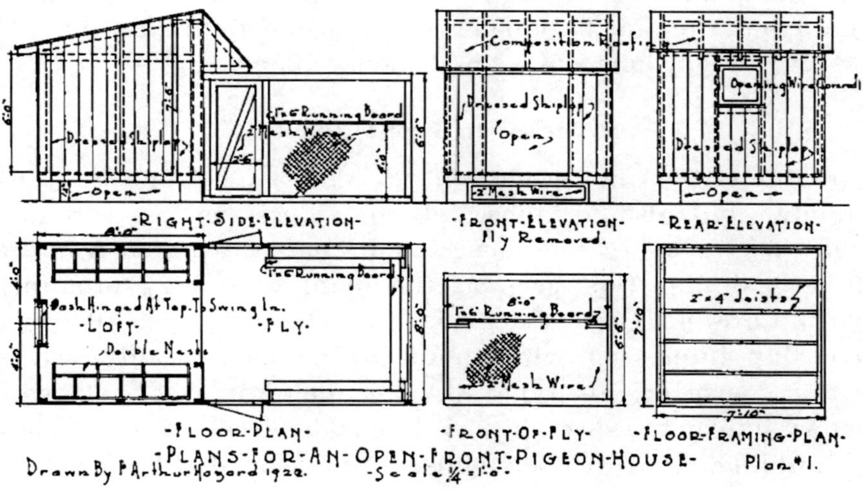

he may use precast concrete blocks, making them 12 in. square and two or three feet long. If wood is to be used I would recommend cypress as it stands moisture better than most woods.

In planning the fly pens I have in every case designed them so that the breeder can catch any bird without much exertion. The idea that a fly should be about fourteen or fifteen feet tall is an exploded one and is fast passing into oblivion. I have tried such ideas and have found them a mistake right from the start. Another thing that will be noticed is that I use running boards exclusively and never the old time ladder.

The ladder makes it hard to catch birds and it also deprives them of a chance to stretch out and sun themselves properly. Then too it will be noticed that I do not allow the birds to have the roof of the house as a sunning and lighting place. It has been found by me, for I have owned lofts of this description, that the action of the pigeon manure on the roofing material is very detrimental, causing the roofing material to become worthless in a short while. Aside from this it is extremely hard to catch birds in a pen where they have access to the roof of the house.

I have published herewith a bill for material for each house that I have planned. I believe this is the first time that this has ever been done with squab house plans.

The Open Front House.

In this type of house we find an almost ideal one for warm climates and also for those where it does not get extremely cold. The idea for this house is one that was gotten from one of very similar type seen at the plant of a very prominent South Carolina Carneau fancier some years ago. Being so favorably impressed with the idea the writer built a three section house of this type and has found it absolutely satisfactory in every respect, in fact, I consider it a hard one to beat. In building my three-pen house I made a slight mistake in that it was made only six feet wide in each section instead of eight as they should have been. In making the working drawings shown here this error has been rectified and I believe this width will be found better.

This type of house admits plenty of fresh air and there is nothing better for pigeons provided there are no drafts. By closing just a part of the front we cut out a draft across the nests yet we leave enough of the front open to admit all of the fresh air that is needed. The hooded roof is a good idea in that it keeps all rain out and if the house should contain more than one pen the breeder can go from one to the other, through the gates, under this hood. This is especially good in rainy weather and serves practically the same purpose as the aisle in other types of houses and yet this hood will not cost near as much as the aisle.

In cold weather where there is danger of the squabs freezing it is a good idea to have a burlap curtain put into the front opening. This curtain can easily be made from feed sacks and nailed up under the high point of the roof and the end allowed

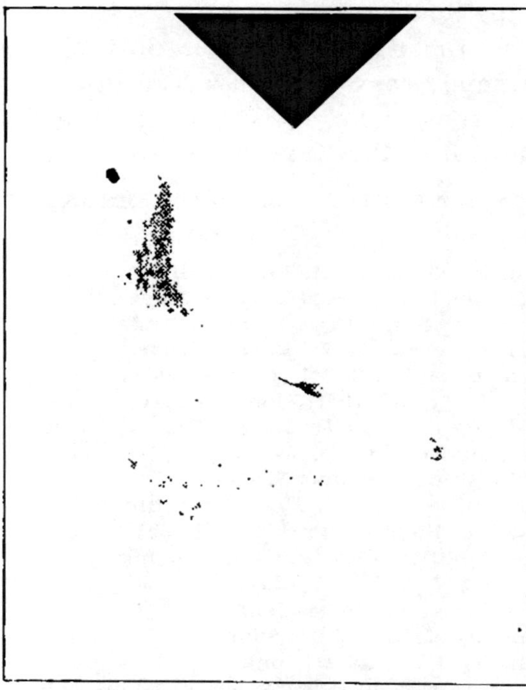

EXCELLENT WHITE KING
Photo from Frank H. Hollmann, Warrenton, Mo.

to rest on the floor on a rod or stick to which the end might be tacked. I have used this curtain very successfully.

There is a saving in the cost of this house over other types in that part of the front is left open and that much lumber is saved and also the lumber that might have been used in constructing the aisle.

Working drawings are shown for a one pen house. To build more of these on either side all that is necessary is to duplicate this one with the exception that between pens we should use two inch mesh wire partitions in behind the nests. Therefore, only two wooden walls are required. I have, however, prepared a drawing showing several of these units built together and which I believe shows clearly what an attractive plant can be made of this type house.

One feature of the fly is that it is only six feet six inches high. It is extremely easy to catch a bird in a fly of this height.

I believe that those who are contemplating building a new pigeon loft would find this type house the proper one to build

BILL OF MATERIAL FOR OPEN FRONT HOUSE

PLAN NO. 1—HOUSE

4 pieces 2 in. by 6 in., 16 ft. long.—Sills.
2 pieces 2 in. by 6 in., 16 ft. long.—Joists.
3 pieces 2 in. by 4 in., 16 ft. long.—Studs.
4 pieces 2 in. by 4 in., 12 ft. long.—Studs.
2 pieces 2 in. by 4 in., 16 ft. long.—Plates.
5 pieces 2 in. by 4 in., 10 ft. long.—Rafters (Long)
2 pieces 2 in. by 4 in., 14 ft. long.—Rafters (Short).
80 ft. B. M. Cull Roofers.—Flooring.
260 ft. B. M. Shiplap.—Side Walls.
160 ft. B. M. Cull Roofers.—Roof Sheathing.
1 24 in. by 24 in. Sash, Glazed, One Light.
2 Rolls Good Quality Composition Roofing.

FLY.

5 pieces 2 in. by 4 in., 10 ft. long.
6 pieces 2 in. by 4 in., 12 ft. long.
1 pieces 2 in. by 4 in., 16 ft. long.
21 Lin. Feet 2 in. Mesh Poultry Wire, 60 in. wide.
15 Lin. Feet 2 in. Mesh Poultry Wire, 48 in. wide.
2 pair 4 in. Strap Hinges.
2 Padlocks, Hasps and Staples to suit.

Two Pen Pigeon House and Fly

For the man who can use a house of medium size and wishes something that will look neat when finished, I think the two-pen house published herewith will fill his wants very nicely.

This house, if built as shown in the accompanying plans will prove to be one that will last a very long time and give excellent service. Each pen has enough double nests to accommodate forty-eight pairs but I would not advise placing more than twenty pairs in any loft if it can be helped. This would allow four extra double nests in each loft.

The house, as shown, is designed for construction in northern or cold climates. The windows may be closed at night and in a short time the animal heat from the forty pairs of birds will

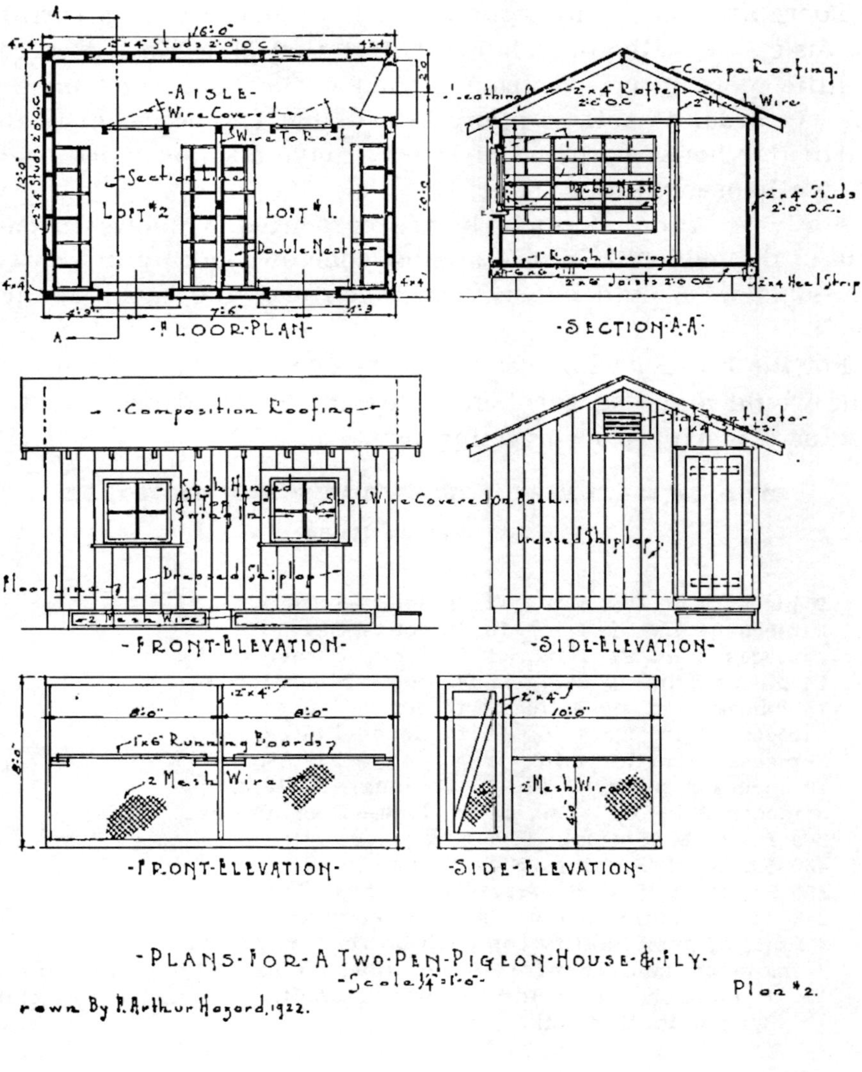

-PLANS-FOR-A TWO-PEN-PIGEON-HOUSE-&-FLY-
-Scale 1/4"=1'-0"-

Plan #2.

rawn By F. Arthur Hazard, 1922.

have the house warm. Of course, the inside sheathing may or may not be used as the owner prefers; I hardly think it would be necessary except in very cold climates.

In planning this house the writer has in some cases shown larger size timbers than are absolutely necessary but I do consider that in order to get a good job the proper size materials must be put into it.

There are some who argue against the house with a corridor or aisle. We all appreciate the fact that this aisle does cost a little more to be constructed than if the house had none at all. In order to suit as many as possible I have designed this particular house with the aisle yet I have also, on other pages, shown houses without same.

For ventilation we have louvre or slatted windows in each end of the gable. To guard against sparrows getting in between the slats we should put a wire screen over the backs of these slats.

For the breeder who does not carry over twenty pairs of birds this would make an excellent house for he could use the other pen as a rearing pen for youngsters.

BILL OF MATERIAL FOR TWO PEN PIGEON HOUSE

Nests Not Included.

HOUSE

2 pieces 4 in. by 6 in., 12 ft. long—Sills.
2 pieces 4 in. by 6 in., 16 ft. long—Sills.
2 pieces 4 in. by 4 in., 14 ft. long—Corner Posts.
14 pieces 2 in. by 6 in., 12 ft. long—Floor Joists.
15 pieces 2 in. by 4 in., 14 ft. long—Studs.
3 pieces 2 in. by 4 in., 16 ft. long—Plates.
3 pieces 2 in. by 4 in., 12 ft. long—Plates.
10 pieces 2 in. by 4 in., 16 ft. long—Rafters.
5 pieces 2 in. by 4 in., 14 ft. long—Door Frames.
200 Ft. B. M. Shiplap—Flooring.
450 Ft. B. M. Shiplap—Side Walls.
300 Ft. B. M. Cull Roofers—Roof Sheathing.
2 36 in. by 36 in. 4-light Sash—Windows.
3 Rolls of good quality composition roofing, 36 Lin. feet.
2 in. mesh poultry wire 48 in. wide. 5 pair 4 in. strap hinges. 1 Padlock, hasp and staples to suit. No inside sheathing **figured in this bill.**

FLY

10 pieces 2 in. by 4 in., 16 ft. long.
6 pieces 2 in. by 4 in., 10 ft. long.
3 pieces 1 in. by 6 in., 14 ft. long.
72 Lin. feet 2 in. mesh poultry wire 48 in. wide. 32 Lin. feet 2 in. mesh poultry wire 60 in. wide. 3 pair of 4 in. strap hinges 2 padlocks, hasps and staples to suit.

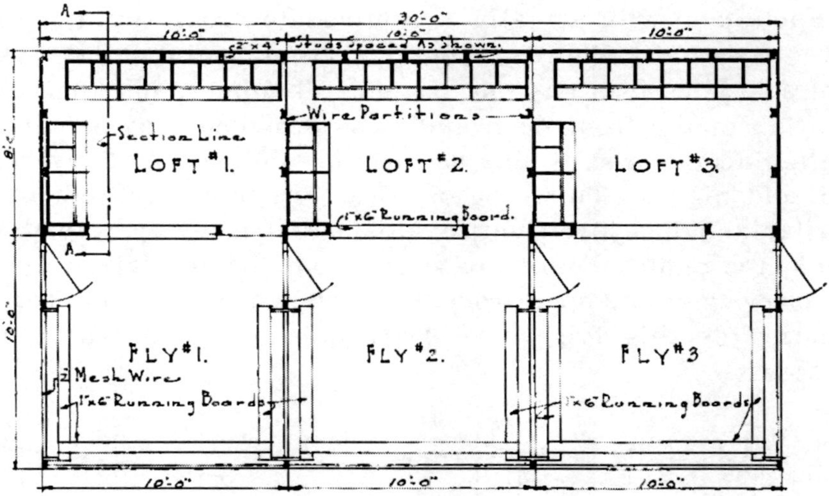

FLOOR PLAN
Scale 1/4"=1'-0"

PLANS FOR A THREE PEN PIGEON HOUSE
Drawn By F. Arthur Hazard 1922.

Plan #3.
Sheet 1.

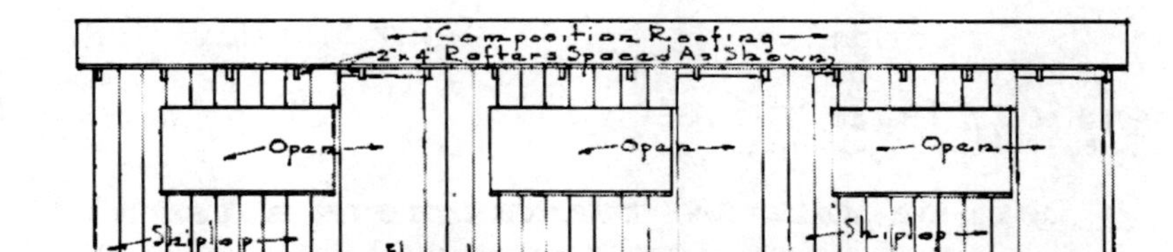

FRONT ELEVATION
Scale 1/4"=1'-0"

PLANS FOR A THREE PEN PIGEON HOUSE
Drawn By F. Arthur Hazard 1922.

Plan #3
Sheet 2.

The Three Pen Pigeon House

We are publishing still another type of open front house or what closely approaches an open front structure. The house can be built in one section or as many sections as may be desired but for convenience we have shown it in the three pen form here.

Each pen will actually accommodate from twenty-four to twenty-six pairs of birds though we recommend that only twenty pairs be housed in any one section. This house has the greater portion of the front open and is so designed that in winter a batten door and sash may be installed to keep the house warm on cold nights. This type of house has been tried out by the writer and has given entire satisfaction in every way though its shape requires more space to accommodate a given number of birds than our open front house shown in plan number one. Houses of this type have been quite popular with pigeon breeders.

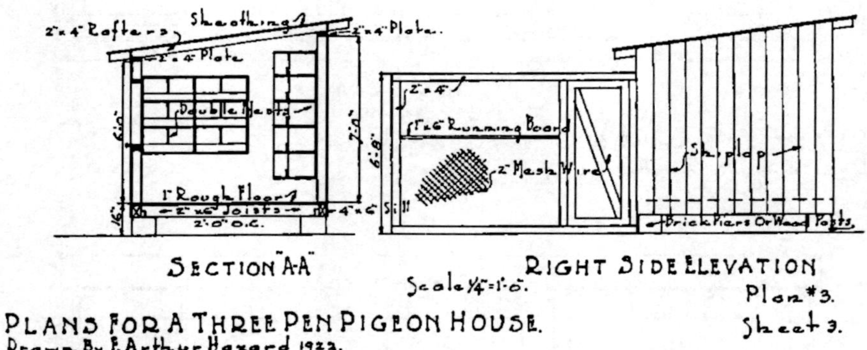

BILL OF MATERIAL FOR THREE PEN HOUSE

PLAN NO. 3—HOUSE

2 pieces 4 in. by 6 in., 8 ft. long—Sills.
6 pieces 4 in. by 6 in., 10 ft. long—Sills.
6 pieces 2 in. by 4 in., 10 ft. long—Heel Strips.
4 pieces 2 in. by 4 in., 12 ft. long—Studs.
11 pieces 2 in. by 4 in., 14 ft. long—Studs.
6 pieces 2 in. by 4 in., 10 ft. long—Plates.
3 pieces 2 in. by 4 in., 12 ft. long—Window Framing.
16 pieces 2 in. by 4 in., 10 ft. long—Rafters.

300 Ft. B. M. 1 in. by various widths rough boards—Flooring.
600 Ft. B. M. Shiplap—Side Walls.
385 Ft. B. M. Cull Roofers—Roof Sheathing.
3 Rolls good quality composition roofing.
28 Lin. feet 2 in. mesh wire 48 in. wide.

FLY

16 pieces 2 in. by 4 in., 10 ft. long.
12 pieces 2 in by 4 in., 12 ft. long.
3 pieces 1 in. by 4 in., 14 ft. long.
3 pieces 1 in. by 4 in., 10 ft. long.
1 piece 1 in. by 4 in., 16 ft. long.
130 Lin. feet 2 in. mesh wire 60 in. wide.
2 Padlocks, hasps and staples to suit.
2 Hooks and eyes.
4 pairs of 4 in. strap hinges.

The Individual Runt Breeding Pen

I am showing a set of working drawings for Individual Runt breeding pens which I trust will fill a long felt want. To my knowledge drawings of this kind have never been presented to pigeon fanciers and breeders prior to this time. Mr. C. R. King, of the King Lofts, Hayward, California, has allowed the writer to model this house after those that he has been using in breeding his famous stud of Runts and the drawings have

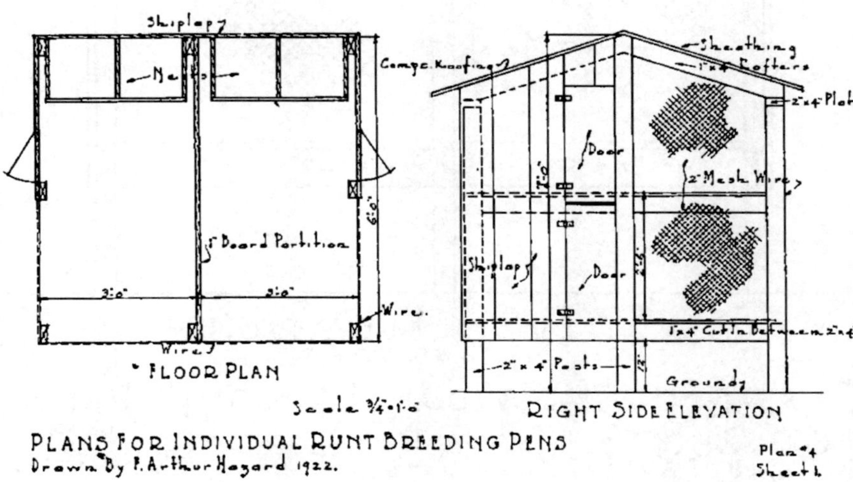

been made as close as possible to his description and photographs of his houses. These seem to be very inexpensive and should prove a great thing for the Runt breeder in that he can keep each pair separately.

On the other hand it appears to the writer that these houses could assist materially in breeding high grade pedigreed birds of any breed.

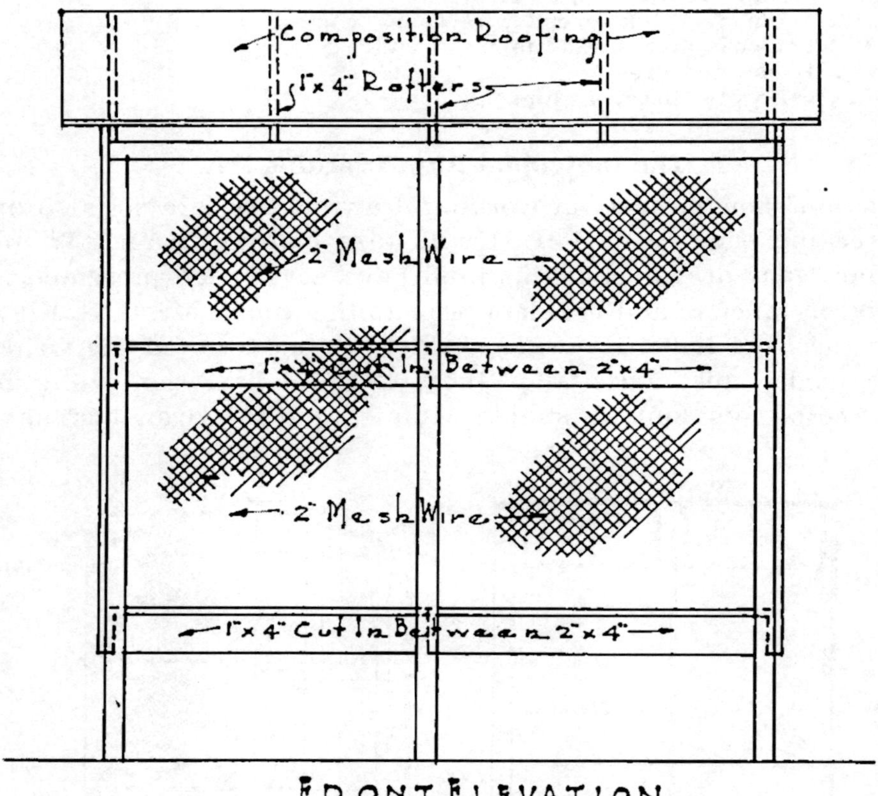

FRONT ELEVATION
Scale 3/4"=1'-0"

PLANS FOR INDIVIDUAL BREEDING PENS FOR RUNTS.
Drawn By F. Arthur Hagard 1922.

Plan #4.
Sheet 2.

BILL OF MATERIAL FOR INDIVIDUAL RUNT BREEDING PENS

3 pieces 2 in. by 4 in., 12 ft. long—Studs.
1 piece 2 in. by 4 in., 14 ft. long—Studs.
1 piece 2 in. by 4 in., 12 ft. long—Plates.
4 pieces 2 in. by 4 in., 12 ft. long—Joists.
5 pieces 1 in. by 4 in., 8 ft. long—Rafters.
90 Ft. B. M. Cull Roofers—Flooring.
45 Ft. B. M. Cull Roofers—Dividing Partition.
80 Ft. B. M. Shiplap—Side Walls.
70 Ft. B. M. Cull Roofers—Roof Sheathing.
1 Roll good quality composition roofing.
24 Lin. feet 2 in. mesh poultry wire 36 in. wide.
4 pair 2 in. strap hinges.
4 Padlocks, hasps and staples to suit.

The Monitor Type Squab House

Some years ago the writer made plans for a ten pen monitor type squab house which has been published in the American Pigeon Journal. I am now presenting another set of drawings for a house of this type but have cut the size down considerably by making the pens only eight feet square instead of ten as I believe this nearer the proper size.

A house of this type is an excellent one in that it gets cross ventilation yet no drafts across the nests. It provides a light airy room for the birds and is not as crowded as some of the

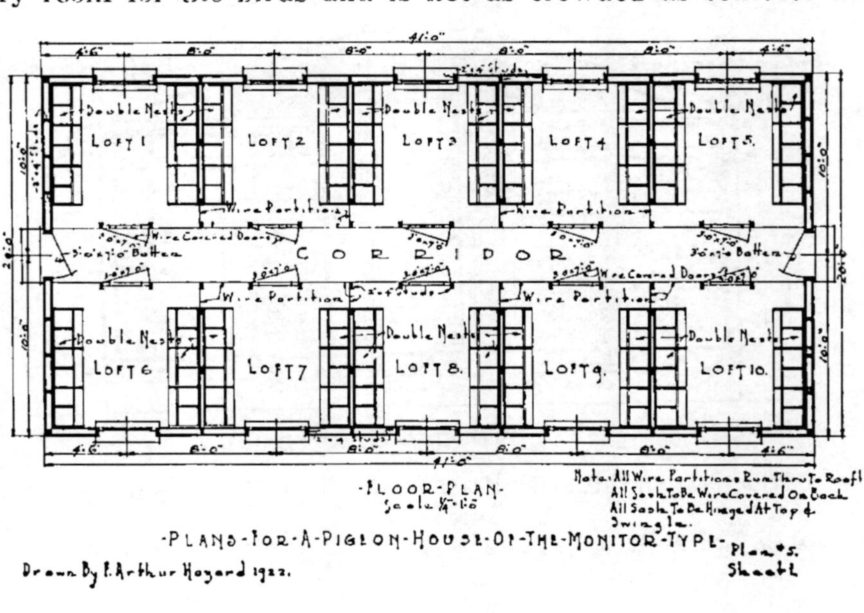

other houses. It makes an ideal house to accommodate around two hundred and fifty mated pairs of pigeons.

I have shown the house sheathed on the inside but have not figured out the necessary sheathing in our bill of material. I do not deem it necessary to have sheathing except in climates where severe winters are had each year. In fact I am opposed to the inside sheathing as it goes toward making a home for rats and mice and they are not at all desired.

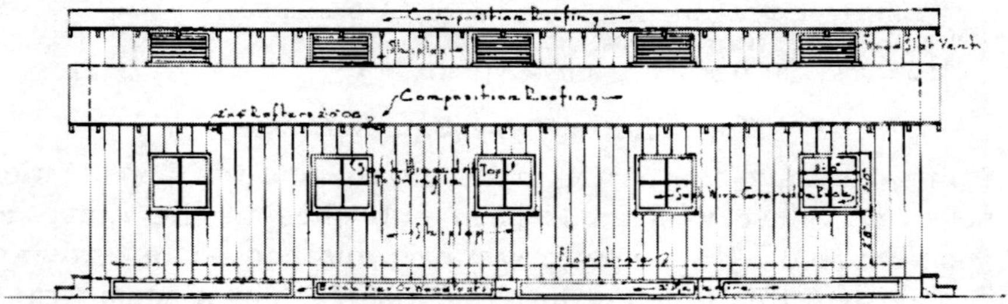

SIDE ELEVATION
Scale ¼"=1'-0"
Opposite Side The Same

PLANS FOR A PIGEON HOUSE OF THE MONITOR TYPE
Drawn By F. Arthur Hazard 1922.

Plan #5.
Sheet 2.

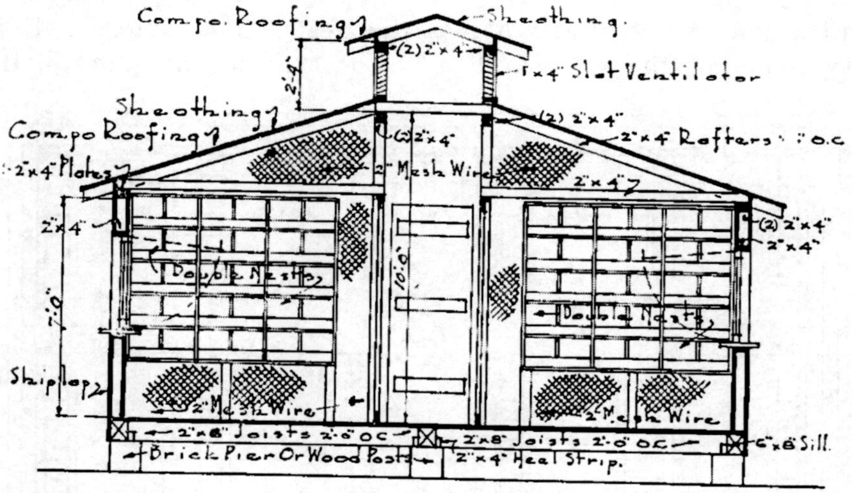

CROSS SECTION

-PLANS-FOR-A-PIGEON-HOUSE-OF-THE-MONITOR-TYPE-
Scale ¼"=1'-0"

Drawn By F. Arthur Hazard 1922. Plan #5. Sheet 3.

BILL OF MATERIAL FOR MONITOR TYPE SQUAB HOUSE

PLAN NO. 5.

13 pieces 6 in. by 8 in., 10 ft. long—Sills.
6 pieces 6 in. by 8 in., 12 ft. long—Sills.
12 pieces 2 in. by 4 in., 10 ft. long—Heel Strips.
8 pieces 2 in by 4 in., 12 ft. long—Heel Strips.
26 pieces 2 in. by 4 in., 10 ft. long—Studs.
26 pieces 2 in. by 4 in., 14 ft. long—Studs.
8 pieces 2 in. by 4 in., 16 ft. long—Studs.
4 pieces 2 in. by 4 in., 12 ft. long—Studs.
574 Lin. ft. 2 in. by 4 in.—Plates.
5 pieces 2 in. by 4 in., 12 ft. long—Window Framing
3 pieces 2 in. by 4 in., 12 ft. long—Door Heads.
10 pieces 2 in. by 4 in., 14 ft. long—Doors (Wire.)
5 pieces 2 in. by 4 in., 12 ft. long—Doors (Wire).
46 pieces 2 in. by 4 in., 10 ft. long—Rafters.
12 pieces 2 in. by 4 in., 12 ft. long—Rafters.
8 pieces 2 in. by 4 in., 10 ft. long—Partition Ties.
1020 Ft. B. M. Shiplap, Cull Roofers or rough square edge boards—Flooring.
1300 Ft. B. M. Cull Roofers—Roof Sheathing.
1400 Ft. B. M. Shiplap—Side Walls.
5 pieces 1 in. by 4 in., 12 ft. long—Slat Vents.
160 Lin. Ft. 2 in. mesh wire 48 in. wide—Cross Partitions.
300 Lin. Ft. 2 in. mesh wire 36 in. wide—Corridor Partitions. and Doors.
30 Lin. Ft. 2 in. mesh wire 36 in. wide—Window Sash.
11 Rolls Composition Roofing.
10 36 in. by 36 in. Sash 4 or 6 lights.
10 pair 2 in. strap hinges. 6 pair 6 in. strap hinges.
10 pair 4 in. strap hinges. 2 Padlocks, hasps and staples to suit.

The Squab Dressing Plant.

In presenting the plans for a squab dressing plant I am confident that it will fill a long felt want and will meet with the approval of the various breeders. The writer has visited many a squab plant but I must say that I have never seen an up-to-date squab dressing plant operated by any of them. To my mind every squab plant of any size should have such a house built and equipped as we have shown as it provides a sanitary place wherein squabs may be made ready for the markets. It provides a place where the work of killing and shipping squabs may be done quickly and economically—where everything is designed and at hand for that purpose.

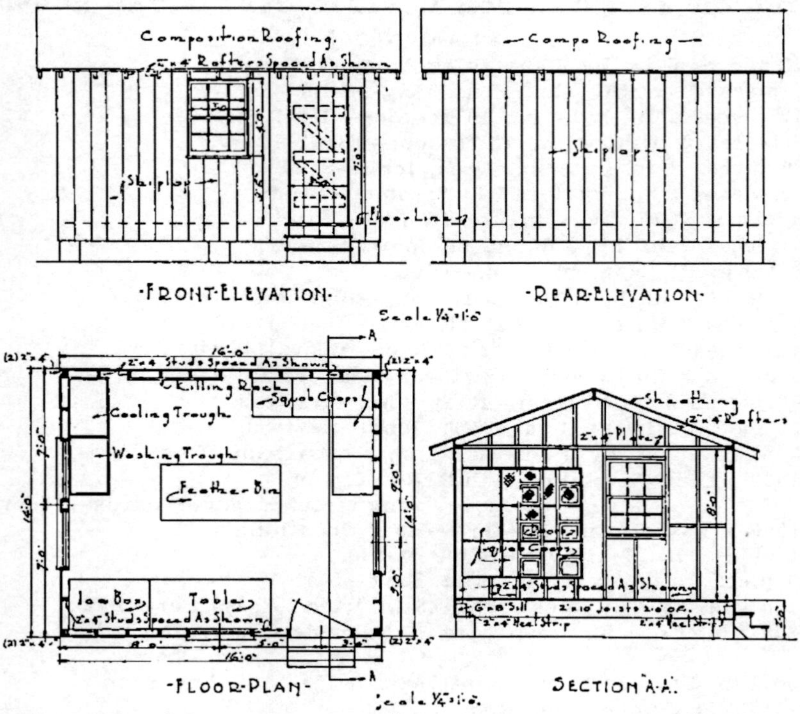

PLANS FOR A SQUAB DRESSING PLANT. Plan #6.
Drawn By F. Arthur Hogard 1922. Sheet 1.

Coops are provided wherein squabs may be kept over night without feeding so that their crops will be empty when killed. Very few plants seem to have such accommodations as this.

A killing rack is built on the wall as shown and is simply a 1 in. by 4 in. board with six penny nails driven at intervals of four inches so that about one-half of each nail is driven in.

A galvanized iron lined wooden trough is built in and divided into two parts. A ¾ in. water pipe is run to each half and provided with two garden hose spigots. These supply the water for cooling and washing the squabs after they are picked.

Next we have a built-in feather bin on the floor over which all squabs are picked. Squab feathers are indeed worth saving as the breast and neck feathers, also those from the rump and thigh, are good for making sofa pillows and can be sold at a good price.

We have an ice box of good size where dressed squabs may be packed and frozen stiff before shipment is made. To do this gives a mighty good start to the squabs on their journey to the markets.

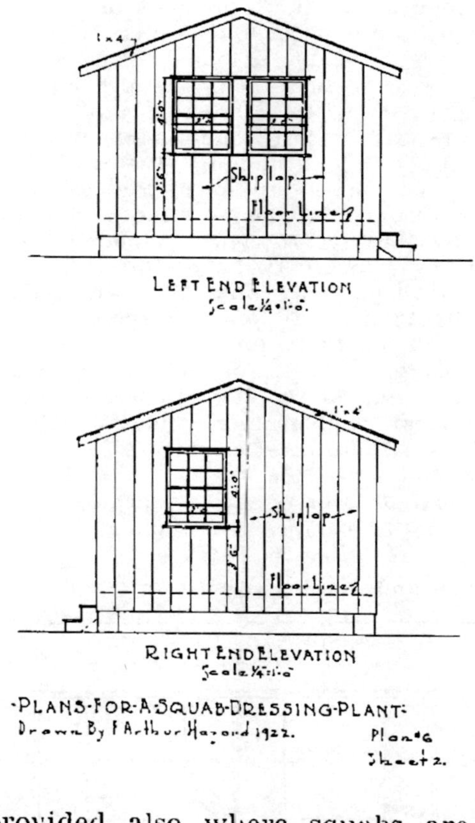

A table is provided also where squabs are wrapped and packed for shipment. On this table is kept a set of scales where each and every squab should be weighed before it leaves the plant.

Thus we have shown how compact and desirable the dressing plant is and how much better it is to have everything at hand in one room where plenty of fresh air and light is to be had.

The writer hopes the time is not far distant when such plants as this one will be very popular.

BILL OF MATERIAL FOR A SQUAB DRESSING PLANT

PLAN NO. 6

2 pieces 6 in. by 8 in., 16 ft. long—Sills.
2 pieces 6 in. by 8 in., 14 ft. long—Sills.
8 pieces 2 in. by 10 in., 14 ft. long—Joists.
2 pieces 2 in. by 4 in., 16 ft. long—Heel Strip.
18 pieces 2 in. by 4 in., 16 ft. long—Studs.
2 pieces 2 in. by 4 in., 12 ft. long—Gable Studs.
2 pieces 2 in. by 4 in., 14 ft. long—Plates.
2 pieces 2 in. by 4 in., 16 ft. long—Platts.
1 piece 2 in. by 4 in., 14 ft. long—Window Framing.
1 piece 2 in. by 4 in., 16 ft. long—Window Framing.
22 pieces 2 in. by 4 in., 10 ft. long—Rafters.
1 piece 2 in. by 10 in., 6 ft. long—Step Stringers.
1 piece 1 in. by 10 in., 6 ft. long—Steps.
1 piece 1 in. by 4 in., 12 ft. long—Window Sills.
4 pieces 1 in. by 4 in., 10 ft. long—Verge Boards.
1 piece 1 in. by 4 in., 14 ft. long—Door Battens.
4 12-light plain rail double hung windows 36 in. by 48 in.
280 Ft. B. M. Cull Roofers—Flooring.
650 Ft. B. M. Shiplap—Side Walls.
400 Ft. B. M. Cull Roofers—Roof Sheathing.
4 Rolls good quality composition roofing.
1 ½ pairs 4 in. strap hinges.
1 Padlock, hasp and staples to suit.

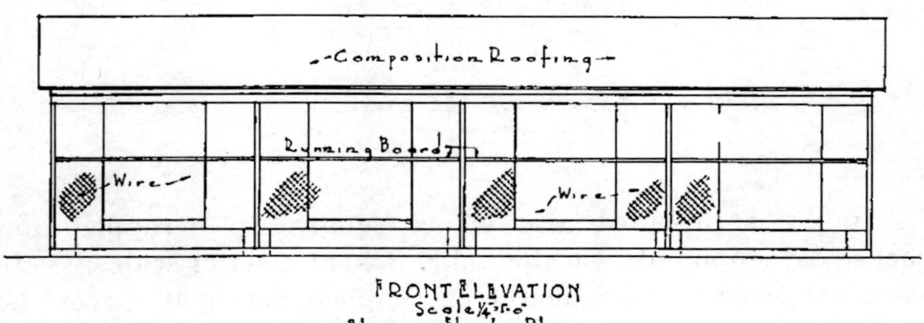

FRONT ELEVATION
Scale ¼"=1'0"
Showing Flys In Place.

FOUR PEN OPEN FRONT PIGEON HOUSE

Drawn By F Arthur Hazard 1922.

Layout of a Plant to Accommodate 1000 Pairs of Pigeons.

When the writer made up his mind to publish this book he decided to endeavor to give his readers something different from the usual things that have been published heretofore and I believe I am publishing herewith something that has never been shown in any other book on the subject of pigeons, at least the writer has never seen it.

I am positive that in the next few years a goodly number of large squab plants will be built. Those who contemplate such as this now have an opportunity of having a well laid-out scheme to work to for I am showing a layout for a modern pigeon plant to house one thousand pairs of breeding birds.

In making this layout I have used my open front house shown on plan number one and have therefore allowed for each loft to accommodate twenty pairs of birds, the fifty lofts therefore accommodating one thousand pairs. The arrangement of the sections permits plenty of sunlight and air around each one.

There has been provided two large youngster pens wherein young stock from the best pairs may be reared each year to take the place of the older birds or to be sold as breeding stock.

At the entrance end of the plant we have a squab dressing plant and a feed house both of which are, of course, essential.

In selecting a plot of ground on which to build a plant one should not overlook a very important point, namely, drainage. Select a dry piece of ground where the drainage will be natural and quick, as sloppy, muddy ground is not at all desirable around a squab plant.

We have dimensioned our layout so that it will be an easy matter for any one to stake out the buildings and then build them by the plans which we have referred to and which are shown elsewhere in this book.

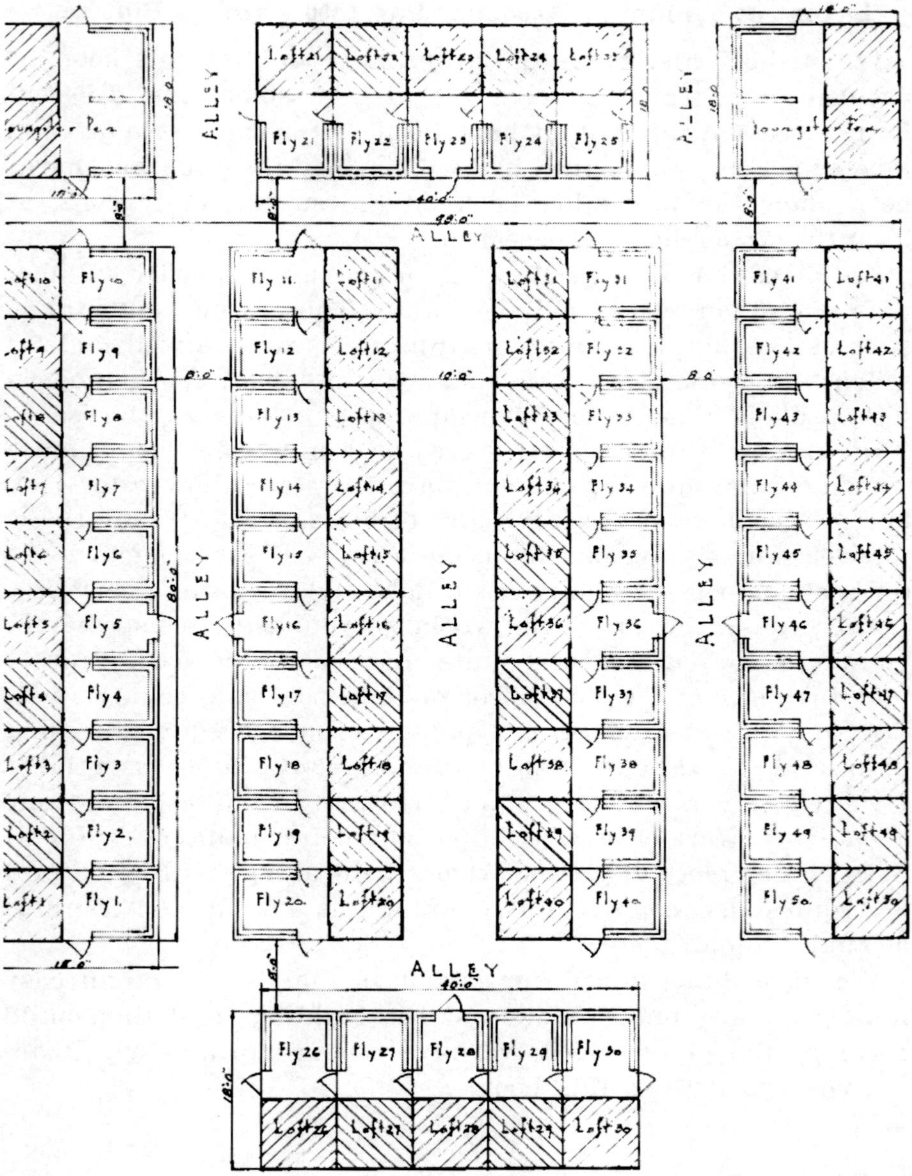

LAYOUT OF A PLANT TO ACCOMODATE 1000 PAIRS OF PIGEONS.

Scale 1/8" = 1'0"

Drawn By F. Arthur Hazard.

CHAPTER VI

WATERING SYSTEMS

Fouled Water—Drinking Fountains—Bathing Pans—Continuous Flow Systems—Explanation of Continuous Flow System.

Pigeons require quite a bit of water for drinking and bathing. Birds that are breeding consume even more because of the fact that they use a large amount in mixing the squab's feed in the crop before this milky substance is disgorged into the throat of the young bird. It is essential therefore that an adequate water supply should be provided. Under no circumstances should water be given to pigeons in an open receptacle for it will soon become fouled and fouled water will do the same thing as fouled grain, namely: cause sickness. In no case should the breeder attempt to supply bathing and drinking water from the same bath pan. The birds will bathe in it and it soon becomes covered with a greasy scum which of course makes it totally unfit for drinking. For the breeder who cannot afford to install an automatic or continuous flow system, it is recommended that he use the most common system of all—the drinking fountain. These can be had at any poultry supply house for a nominal price and will last a long time. They are made of galvanized iron in sizes from one pint on up to several gallons, the one gallon size probably being the best suited for the average pen of birds. These fountains protect the water from being fouled and if thoroughly washed in boiling water once a week will be sanitary in every way.

Use an ordinary dishpan for furnishing baths for the birds. The size best suited for this is one about five inches deep and from eighteen inches to twenty inches in diameter. A bath should be given in these pans every day or two when the weather conditions permit.

It is practical economy to install a continuous flow system in the plant just as soon as possible for it is certainly a labor saver in every way. This system provides an ever fresh supply of water and usually can be regulated so as to consume but very little water.

The writer has prepared a drawing for a constant flow fountain which I know will give entire satisfaction if properly installed and one on which the first cost is the last. There are

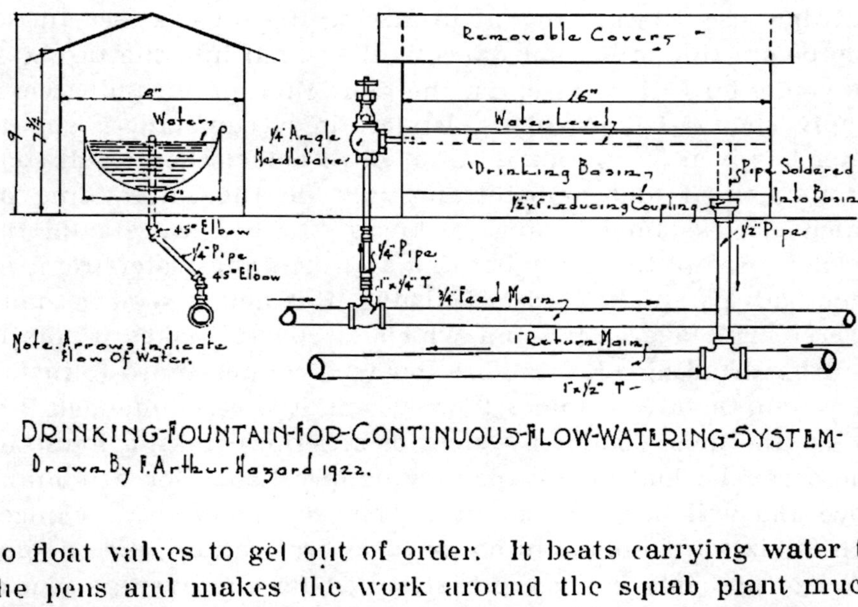

DRINKING-FOUNTAIN-FOR-CONTINUOUS-FLOW-WATERING-SYSTEM-
Drawn By F. Arthur Hazard 1922.

no float valves to get out of order. It beats carrying water to the pens and makes the work around the squab plant much more pleasant, in short it does away with a certain amount of drudgery and provides clean cool water for the birds to drink.

Where the ground on which the plant is located slopes, due allowance must be made to take care of the grade and the pen containing the last fountain on the overflow line must be the highest one so that the water will properly drain back to the sewer if necessary to drain the overflow water back in the direction where the main supply starts. The water in the feed pipe will very naturally flow upwards because of the fact that it has pressure behind it.

Let me explain this system. By the use of a two pipe system we get a main feed pipe and a return main. Each fountain is connected to the feed main and to the return main independently of the other fountains. One may shut the valves off at any fountain and not disturb the flow to any other fountain at any time. This is a decided advantage. Where the system is installed and ready for use we turn on a control valve at the junction of the supply main and the main from the street, having previously opened up each angle needle valve at the fountains so that there will be a constant drip into the fountains. The fountains fill up in due course of time and as they do so the overflow pipes start to function and carry off the surplus water. These fountain valves can be so regulated that it will be impossible to overflow a fountain. Thus there is a never ceasing flow of water in the system through the fountains at all times until we cut off the control valves. In this way a fresh cool and clean supply of water is ever before the birds.

By the construction of these fountains the birds cannot foul the water in any way whatsoever as they cannot get to the water only to drink it.

The feed and return mains should be buried from twelve to eighteen inches according to the freezing depth in any locality.

The fountain is so constructed that it can be lifted away from the supply pipe and up from the return pipe in order that we can take it out and scald it thoroughly. This is a mighty good idea. Then too, by removing the fountain as I have just mentioned, there are no connections to be loosened with a wrench, we can slip the bath pan under the supply pipe and fill it for the bath.

It is my opinion that this system will be a great help to any breeder that can install it. It should not cost so very much at this time, for the plumbing materials necessary for its installation have gone down in price considerably.

CHAPTER VII

MATING

Subject Worthy of Much Consideration—Two Methods, Natural and Forced, Discussed.

This is probably one of the most important subjects connected with pigeon breeding and surely one that is worthy of a great deal of consideration both by the inexperienced and the experienced breeder. To my mind it is one of the points concerning the breeding of pigeons that we can always learn something about and yet we invariably find very little attention paid to it among a great many breeders especially among owners of commercial squab plants.

Dr. A. F. Whelan, the noted Maltese breeder of Kansas City, makes a very emphatic and true statement in his article, "High Class Maltese Second to None," in the American Pigeon Journal, May 1920, issue, when he says: "Mating properly is half of the battle, the stock is the other half." There was never a truer statement, concerning pigeons, put into print than this one. The progeny of the best stock in the world may be ruined and made totally unfit for breeding if they are carelessly mated year after year. Yet how often we see breeders going on indefinitely allowing their stock to mate up promiscuously, trusting to sheer luck that the result will prove a happy one.

There are two methods of mating pigeons. One is what is termed the natural mating and the other is what is known as forced mating. We will first discuss the natural system. The breeder places a few cocks and hens in one pen and allows them to remain there together for a week or ten days. The desire to mate being born in the birds they will very naturally begin to select their mates and pair off and will soon start billing and cooing and very probably start a nest. They have, therefore, mated just as they would have done had they never been confined but of that class that fly at large. We allow them to go ahead with their first set of eggs and during this time we study each pair carefully to see that they are properly suited to each other to produce the best results possible. If they are so suited we catch them one by one and place the proper leg bands on

LACED WING OR SPANGLED POLISH LYNX
Photo from Edwin W. Knowles, Baltimore, Md.

their legs, giving each pair a different numbered band from any other pair and enter, on our records, the numbers on the bands and the parentage record. For example: Suppose we number a pair twelve white. Suppose that the cock bird in this pair was bred from pair twenty-six yellow and the hen from fifteen blue. These numbers are entered on the record sheets for our new pair twelve white and this information at once establishes the parentage record. In all cases we band the cock on the right leg and the hen on the left one. On the other hand suppose we find a pair mated that are not suited to each other in that they are both weak in the same sections. We should remember that when two birds with the same weakness

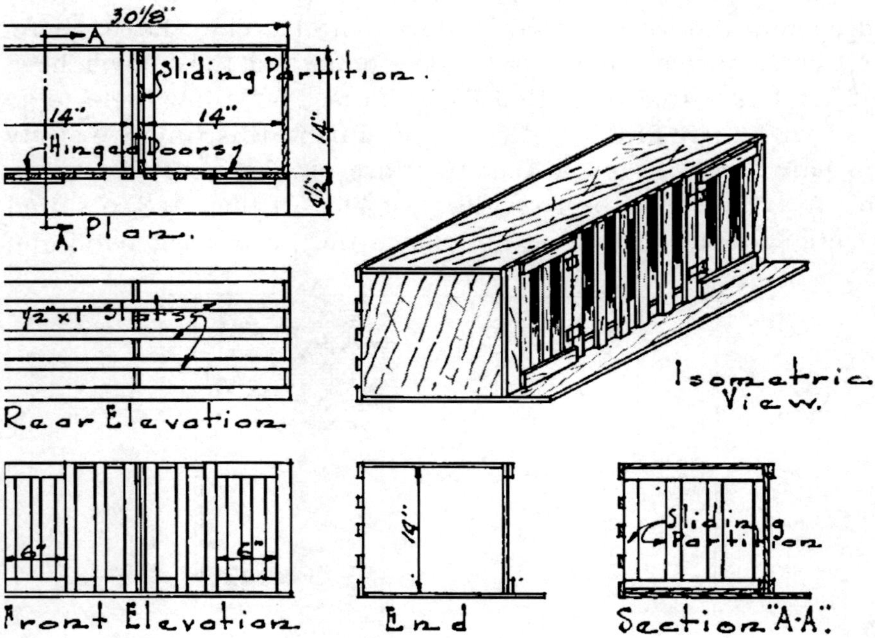

ATING COOP.
awn By F. Arthur Hazard 1922.

red together the weakness is intensified in the progeny ve should, therefore, break this mating up at once and e either the cock or the hen from the pen.

ed mating is perhaps the best method of mating that can d but, of course, requires equipment to carry it out. The nent breeders and I might say those that get the best s are the ones that use this system. If any birds are to ated several mating coops should be made and kept on at all times. I am publishing herewith working drawings coop of this kind which will prove to be inexpensive. The r that finds he has a good hen that is not mated will around in his lofts and very probably notice a cock that if mated to this hen, throw some excellent youngsters. erefore, catches both birds and places one in either side of the mating coop. Here he supplies them with grain, water and health grit, having only one container for the grain so that in eating they will get accustomed to each other. If these birds fight at first separate them, moving one or the other to another coop for a day. Put them back together at the expiration of this time and let them remain there together for a few days, never putting the two birds in the same side of the coop. As a general rule the two birds so treated will mate. If you see them kissing and billing through the slatted partition you may then put them in the "Test Pen," and allow them to start to work. Watch them closely and should they not start building a nest in a few days try them in the mating coop again or search for other birds to mate them with. If, however, they go to work when placed in the "Test Pen" let them raise a pair of squabs, band them properly and then place them in the breeding lofts or sell them as you may wish. Before selling young mated pairs of this kind we would advise letting them raise more than one pair of squabs so that you may make sure that they are really mated correctly and ready to be sold.

If, for any reason, a mated pair in the breeding lofts do not work so well together try remating them with other birds by using the mating coop, the cock with a strange hen and the hen with a strange cock bird. Sometimes this will work very nicely.

In mating pigeons, we can, with the use of a little patience, secure proper coloring, correct size and breed them to a standard but it must be done with some reason back of it all. Suppose we have a breed whose standard calls for a well rounded skull. We have an excellent cock bird that is strong in skull section and weak in breadth of back and we also have a hen with a very wide back and not so good a skull section. If these two birds are mated together we will get one or two youngsters that will be a happy medium. However, were either of these birds mated to others that were weak in the same sections our time would have been wasted for the youngsters very likely inherit the same defects and probably be worse than the parents in the defective sections or section because we have not mated the birds so that we may overcome the defect. Therefore, in order to improve our stock we must use this method of mating at all times. Careless and incorrect mating will avail nothing and time will be wasted.

Of course we must apply the same method of mating when we are breeding for color. To get the proper color in pigeons very often requires the most careful study on the part of the breeder. Let nothing escape your attention when summing up the results from your matings, but be very observant and use reasoning. If you do not obtain the desired coloring in one mating go at it again and in other ways until you do succeed. This feature of the business requires perseverance but it is the only method by which you can attain your goal. Color in birds that are producing squabs strictly for commercial purposes does not amount to very much but it does in birds that are bred for exhibition.

CHAPTER VIII

BANDING

Types of Leg Bands—Recording Band Numbers—Seamless Bands—Open Bands.

Leg bands of some description are almost a necessity in the well regulated and modern pigeon plant, be it small or large. It is with the aid of these little markers that we know mated pairs, the lofts in which they belong and the parentage of the squabs, etc.

There are two types of leg bands, namely: the seamless band and the open band. The seamless band is usually made of thin aluminum and is, as the name implies, made without a seam. This band is placed on the squab's leg during the first six or eight days of its life and it is the mark by which the age, parentage, etc., of the squab may be told at any future date. To apply this band take the toes of the squab on one foot and close them together, then slip the band over the toes up on to the leg. Care should be taken to get the band on before the foot and leg of the squab gets too large. This band should bear a serial number and may also bear the initials of the owner and above all the year date. On more valuable specimens a band manufactured for and sold by the American Pigeon Club or the National Pigeon Association should be used as most shows require all young birds to wear these bands before they will be allowed to enter competition.

Having banded the squab a record is made immediately of the number, showing on the record entry what the numbers of the parents are, the date the squab was hatched, etc. Later on as the sex of the squab becomes known it is entered on the records for future reference.

Seamless bands serve other purposes as well. They can be relied upon to prove ownership in case a bird is stolen. In case a bird is sold a complete description can be given of the bird wearing a certain number band and the purchaser is given a chance to see that he is getting the bird as represented by the seller. If a breeder makes a good win at a show and is offered a handsome sum for a certain prize bird and wishes to

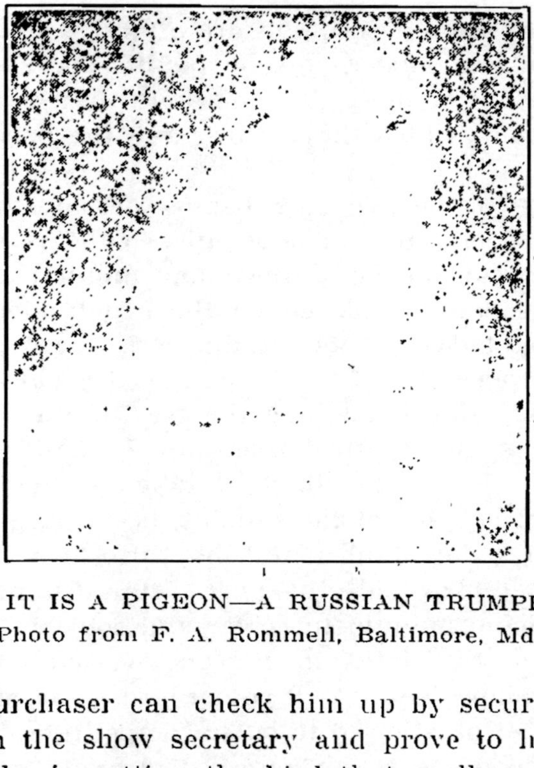

YES, IT IS A PIGEON—A RUSSIAN TRUMPETER
Photo from F. A. Rommell, Baltimore, Md.

sell it the purchaser can check him up by securing the band number from the show secretary and prove to his own satisfaction that he is getting the bird that really won. It tends to make dealings more satisfactory in every way.

The open band is usually made of aluminum and celluloid. The best known bands of this kind are the Bourne "Bignum." The E-C-Z, The Easy On and Coloroid. These bands come in an assortment of colors and in a wide range of numbers. Each pen should have a certain color allotted to it and all birds in that pen banded with bands of this color. The male bird is banded on the right leg and the female on the left leg. The reason for having a different color band for each pen is to enable the breeder to get a bird back into his correct pen should one get out. Each pair wears a different numbered band in all cases. These bands are the means by which the breeding records are kept. No birds should be allowed to remain unbanded at any time. The breeder that does not keep his birds accurately banded can never hope to keep his records straight.

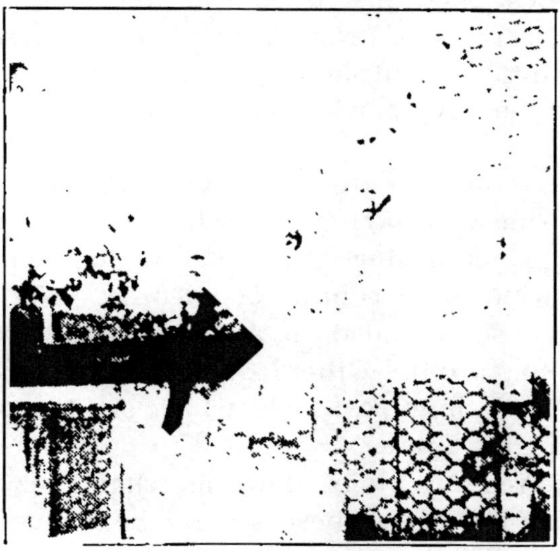

MODENA
Photo from H. W. Barnett, Oakland, Calif.

CHAPTER IX

SYSTEMATIC AND ACCURATE RECORD KEEPING

Showing up Profit Makers and Drones—Record Sheets—Record of Every Pair will be Wanted—Records Valuable in Showing Results of Mating—Exhibition Records.

One of the most essential duties of a breeder is to install and keep systematic records. Not only must a general record be kept of certain pairs but he must have true information at hand to show positively what each and every pair of birds is producing.

To realize a return on the investment we must know what part of the business is paying and what part is not. The only method in the pigeon business by which we can do this is to keep careful and accurate accounts or records. Not all pigeons produce enough squab meat in a year to pay for their keep and return some profit. Others do this. An accurately kept set of records will show positively which are the profit makers and which are the drones.

I have prepared drawings showing what I believe to be a very good record sheet. These should be printed on a good quality of paper, the breeding record being on one side of the sheet and the youngster record on the other side. Have them printed in sheets to fit a nice loose leaf binder and you have the very thing for this purpose. Each pair in the plant, therefore, has its own record for one year right where the breeder can see it at a glance. Then too he knows exactly what becomes of the offspring of this pair, what bands they wear, to what birds they are mated and where to look for the breeding record of each of the youngsters after they have mated. A glance at our record sheet and we find exactly where each bird came from. It shows just how many squabs were killed, saved and banded, etc. Thus at the end of the year we see just what any and every pair is doing. If any particular pair has raised ten pairs of squabs we know they are money makers and we save them for that purpose. If any particular pair shows a total of only four pairs of squabs we know that they are drones and we do not want them so we apply the hatchet and make a note of it on the record sheet. Suppose a pair lays two eggs every

POLISH LYNX
Photo from H. W. Barnett, Oakland, Calif.

month except four and only one or two eggs hatch but our records show no note of broken eggs. We see at a glance that something is wrong and we investigate. If both birds are apparently all right we remate them to find out where the trouble is. In this way we get right down to hard boiled facts because we must have these facts in order to know what birds are the profitable ones. There is no argument against systematic records. The man who does not keep them cannot tell what his birds are doing. He might be able to tell you how many squabs his two hundred pairs produced in one year and how much he sold them for and what his profit was but he cannot tell you which birds made the profit and which ones helped to keep him from making more. He will tell you he does not want those which helped to reduce his profits but he cannot help himself because he does not know what birds they are. Had he kept accurate records he would know immediately the true facts in the case. It is the breeder who watches these details that succeeds. Efficiency counts here as well as elsewhere. Give the hard workers a chance. Get rid of your drones and build your flock up to a high standard—higher than your neighbor and your stock will make a name for you.

The time is not far distant when the wise buyer will ask for a record of every pair of birds he buys and if you do not keep records you will lose many a sale. One important move has already been made in that direction and I for one, earnestly hope to see it become more general. It will gradually eliminate or at least go a long way to help eliminate the crooked men in the business.

Aside from the breeding record as regards the number of squabs produced we may look upon our records in another light. Let us go into our youngster pen and pick out a certain bird. We notice the leg band and upon turning to our record we soon find out what pair it came from. We compare this bird with the parents. Here, my dear reader, is where you get an unmistakable answer to what has the pair produced. Then see the result—a living thing produced from two living things you mated together to produce. Have you attained your goal? What was the result of your mating? You have a living reply. You now know definitely that this pair did or did not produce a certain type, that they did or did not produce a desired color, that they did or did not produce your long wished for size, feather or bone. What proves all of this to you? There is but one answer and that is "Systematic and Accurate Record Keeping." Do not be content with comparing one youngster with its parents. Turn to your valuable records once more and get the leg band number of another or several more youngsters from

RECORD OF YOUNGSTERS.

Band No.	Mated To	Date	Sex	Sold.	To Whom Sold	Record Page

REMARKS:-

BREED____________

Pen No.________ Pair No.______ Band Color______ Date Mated______

Cock-Seamless Band No.________ Hen-Seamless Band No.______

Description Of Cock______________________________

Description Of Hen______________________________

Band No. Cock's Sire.____________ Band. No. Cock's Dam.______

Band No. Hen's Sire.____________ Band No. Hen's Dam.______

BREEDING RECORD

Month	Eggs Layed	Date	Hatched	Date	Killed	Band No.	Date	Remarks
January								
February								
March								
April								
May								
June								
July								
August								
September								
October								
November								
December								
Total								

Sold To____________ Date.________ Price.______

EXHIBITION RECORD______________________________

REMARKS______________________________

this particular pair. Compare these and study the results of your matings. It is beyond the comprehension of the writer how so many breeders can go on year after year and keep no records at all.

Another point while we are on the subject of record keeping. Let us look at our record sheet again and if we want to know what bird of ours won at a certain show we can find it written there before us. Even an exhibition record is kept to tell us in black and white what our birds are doing.

To the breeders who keep no records at all and who flounder around in the dark let me say that you are making a very serious mistake if you do not keep them. It makes no difference if you are a past master at mixing and properly balancing pigeon feeds, whether or not you know best in the world how to market squabs, etc., unless you know what each and every pair of your birds are doing you cannot truthfully say which are desirables and which are non-desirables, and you cannot find out these things without the proper records. If your plant is not paying by all means install records at once and get to the very bottom of things. Remember that the man who succeeds never lets anything stand in his way to overcome that which holds him back in business. Install a system of records and find the trouble and then act accordingly.

I wonder how many of us realize what made the two hundred egg hen? The author can well remember when she was an unheard of thing. Proper feeding and handling did a great deal but I am inclined to think that the trap nest did the major part of it. This trap nest showed its owner which hen laid and which one did not. Records were kept also and between the two the large egg yielders were selected and bred from and in turn their daughters were trapnested and recorded and with the invaluable assistance of records we have thousands of two hundred egg hens in America today with the breeders working hard for the three hundred egg hen. What systematic records have done for poultry it will do for pigeons—it will pick the profit producers and show up the drones.

CHAPTER X

MOULTING

Explanation of the Moult—Separation of Males and Females During the Moult—Care During the Moulting Period.

There is a period in each year when all of the feathered tribe shed their feathers and take on new ones. This process of shedding is natural and is what is known as moulting. The moult comes during the last of the summer months and it is during this time that the birds undergo a terrible bodily strain. Therefore, every precaution should be taken, on the part of the breeder, to keep his birds in the very best condition possible at this season of the year. The writer has always been very liberal in feeding hemp seed and golden millet during the moult and has found these two grains of great value in toning up the birds.

Some breeders advise the separation of the males and females during the moult, preferring to keep them from breeding during this time. This may well be practiced on a small scale but where one is operating a large commercial squab plant it would be unwise indeed to attempt such a thing. Not all birds will breed during the moult but those that do should be carefully cared for and not stinted in their feed.

The first feathers to be moulted are usually the wing feathers, then the tail feathers and lastly the body feathers. During the moult a pigeon, like a chicken, usually presents a most unsightly appearance but the novice need not be alarmed as this is nature's method of giving each bird a new set of feathers.

During the moult the birds should receive more than usual attention. Their lofts should be kept in a sanitary condition, plenty of fresh health grit provided, a lump of rock salt should be on the ground of every fly and a bath should be made ready for the birds every day. A good tonic for the birds during the moult is gentian which should be placed in the drinking water about twice a week. Care should be taken to see that the birds receive food that is especially high in protein at this time.

SEVERAL PENS OF WHITE KINGS, SILVER KINGS, HORUNEAUX AND CRESTED MONDAINES

Photo from Paul Weyer, Elmhurst, Calif.

CHAPTER XI

PRINCIPLES AND PRACTICES OF PIGEON BREEDING

Principles—Variation—Atavism—Contamination—Prepotency—Like Begets Like—Practices—Vigor—Building up a Strain—Inbreeding—Line Breeding—Line Breeding Chart—Description of Line Breeding Chart—Line Breeding as Affecting Squab Producing Birds—Out-Crossing.

PRINCIPLES

In breeding pigeons we should not be content with just mating up our birds or allowing them to mate promiscuously. There are certain principles pertaining to breeding which apply to pigeons and which effect both our natural and forced matings. We should study these principles, watch them work out in our lofts and make use of them or try to overcome their ill effects as the case may be. By doing so we can accomplish much toward bettering our stock. Apparently the breeding of pigeons is an easy task and some are content to believe this. However, to produce high grade specimens is not such an easy matter, if it were, everyone could and probably would do so. But if the breeders would breed their birds along more definite lines and not trust to sheer luck our show rooms would be filled with far superior specimens and our commercial squab plants would ship far better squabs to market than they are now doing.

In making a careful study of this subject I believe that the following are the most important principles that we are concerned with in pigeon breeding:

1. Variation.
2. Atavism.
3. Contamination.

4. Prepotency.
5. Like Begets Like.

I have not attempted to elaborate on this subject but have set forth a few short explanations of the above principles as I understand them and these should be of some help to the novice and the older breeder alike.

VARIATION: In speaking of variation as applied to the breeding of pigeons we mean the difference between the youngsters of the same pair of birds and the difference between the youngsters and their parents. We appreciate the fact that a pair of pigeons does not always throw the same size youngsters, the same shaped youngsters, and in the colored breeds is this especially true as regards the color of the offspring. For example we know that Carneaux do not always throw the same shade of red or yellow in their offspring, the color ranging from a light shade to a darker one. Sometimes this variation is very slight, sometimes it is very pronounced. Not long ago I visited the plant of a breeder who showed me a pair of Kings that at times would throw a clean leg squab and a feathered leg squab in the same nest and again both squabs would be clean leg ones. Of course in a great many pairs we do not find the principle of variation working to so marked a degree.

Again we see the variation in the youngsters as compared with the parents. We may see this in type, color, size, etc. The youngsters may differ to a marked degree in type and be either better or worse in this than either of the parents. They may be lighter or darker in shade of coloring than the parents. Variation is one principle in breeding that allows us to overcome faults in some birds and on the other hand it is one of chief reasons why we have to cull so closely. When we select specimens which show a marked variation for the better then we are on the right road because we are realizing our hope of building up our stock.

ATAVISM: By atavism is meant a reversion or breeding back. Here we find certain faults appearing in the offspring that were prevalent in their ancestry though distantly removed or several generations back in the line. It does not necessarily mean just back to the parents but even on back to the great great grandparents. As an example of this we see the White Kings with feathers on their legs and sometimes after carefully investigating the matter we find that their parents were clean leg specimens. These feathers come from related specimens several generations back in the line yet a majority of White Kings show clean legs and we breed them to get such legs.

CONTAMINATION: In breeding pigeons there is very little chance, if any, for contamination due to the fact that pigeons mate in pairs and remain so mated as long as they live unless they are separated by man. They are faithful to their mates and in my experience I have but once known or seen a female of a mated pair of pigeons receive service from a male other than her mate. In this case both birds were of the same breed. For contamination to take place in pigeons the male and female must be of different breeds or varieties. Such contamination as this would of course result in a cross-bred offspring. There is no need of worry on the part of the breeder concerning contamination in pigeons as long as he keeps unmated pairs of different breeds separated.

PREPOTENCY: This is one of the principles of breeding about which we rarely ever see anything written or scarcely ever hear of in connection with pigeons. Certainly there are prepotent pigeons. In other words there are certain specimens in every loft of any size which have that power of transmitting to or stamping on their offspring certain characteristics. For example: There are birds which excell in breeding qualities and if they have the power to transmit these qualities to their offspring then we would say that they are prepotent in that respect. The degree in which birds are prepotent of course varies. We might have birds that are excellent in color and which transmit this quality to only a few of their offspring. These birds are prepotent in a lesser degree. On the other hand we might have birds which are excellent in color which transmit this quality to the greater portion of their offspring. These are highly prepotent. Again we may have a bird which is prepotent in more than one respect, the writer has seen this time after time. Thus we see of what value prepotency is and the minute we find we have a prepotent bird we should by all means keep him because it is indeed a valuable specimen.

LIKE BEGETS LIKE: This is very probably the most heard of principle in breeding. It is very probably also the most misunderstood of all. A great many novices believe it in its true sense. Herein is where they are wrong and not at all unlikely they are wrong because of the fact that they have been misinformed. For instance, it is a well known fact that the offspring strongly resembles the parents and yet not wholly so. Here is where the principle of variation and that of atavism come into play and upset the "Like Begets Like" theory. There are variations that happen along for some reason and keep the youngsters from being exactly like their parents; there is the tendency to breed back and out crops some defect brought down from past generations. White Runts will produce youngsters that are White Runts true enough and the offspring will have the breed and variety characteristics but in all cases the youngsters from them are not altogether like the parents. So it is with other breeds and varieties. It is a proved fact that both male and female exert an influence on the offspring and it is because of this fact that we cannot carry out this principle of breeding in its true sense of meaning for both male and female are unlike, even though in minor points, and as long as they are different from each other the offspring will be different. Like begets like simply means, after all is said, that the offspring inherits enough of the breed and variety resemblance to be of that breed and variety and will never be an exact reproduction of either male or female. If this theory of like begets like were true in the broadest meaning it would be easy in a way to produce good birds from good birds all the time but on the other hand we would have no variation and therefore no chance to improve the quality of our stock.

PRACTICES

Just as there are certain principles of breeding so are there certain practices. These practices are for the purpose of making use of the principles which have good effects upon the breeding of our birds and for the elimination of the bad effects of the others. Knowing or understanding the various principles we should use such practice in breeding our birds that will enable us to produce superior specimens. In other chapters I have touched upon certain branches of breeding separately and have devoted a whole chapter to each of these branches because of their importance.

VIGOR: In the practice of breeding pigeons, as in breeding poultry, dogs or whatever else we might undertake, there is one thing that I might call paramount. It is VIGOR. I firmly believe that all of my readers will agree that it is essential because we must have strength and vigor in the bird so that it can respond to our experiments. Diseased birds cannot and will not produce as they should, they have not the bodily strength to do so. Therefore we cannot use them or, I might say, we should not use them at any time. The health of the birds should be kept intact, nothing should be done to impair their bodily strength and on the other hand everything possible should be done to build it up. The more vigor a bird has the more pliable he is, that is he will respond better and quicker to severe breeding tests, he will produce more and better offspring provided, of course, he is properly mated. Do not allow yourself to go color mad or type crazy to obtain color or type and sacrifice the vigor of your birds. Do not use a bird that shows excellent type but which at the same time shows little or no "pep" just for the sake of hoping to reproduce that type in a youngster because the chances are that you will get a youngster of less stamina or vigor and with not as much type as his sire or dam. Make vigor your first consideration and then breed for type, color, cere, etc., and you will find these easier to obtain.

BUILDING UP A STRAIN: By a strain is meant a more or

less individual family of a certain breed or variety. To build up a strain is not such an easy task as some are inclined to think for it takes time, forethought, energy and one must apply the soundest breeding practices. Some novices will purchase a few pair of birds and as soon as they have raised a few youngsters and mated them they offer these birds for sale as of a certain strain, giving them a name which is usually that of their owner such as Fred Smith Strain of Homers. This is not a strain. What individuality have they? Probably none; no outstanding feature at all very likely. Strains are not made in one generation nor two but they are made from several of them wherein the breeder has sought for and has accomplished some one or two things which will make his birds stand out pre-eminently. Do not misunderstand me. I do not mean that he has gone so far as to create a new type of bird nor a new color in his birds because if he were to do this he would go further than to build up a strain, his newly made type would not fit the standard for the breed nor would the color. That is not what is desired at all. What he has done when he has made up a strain is that he has selected certain specimens that are within the limits of the standard and which possess to a more or less marked degree certain desired characteristics and has, by careful line breeding, improved these characteristics until they stand out pre-eminently. Certain strains are noted for excellent type, which is handed down from one generation to another; others for excellent color, others for good ceres, etc. Having bred such birds that are traceable back to a few and which have been bred with no introduction of new blood he has established what is known as a strain.

INBREEDING: Inbreeding is the breeding together of birds which are related either closely or distantly. Some think that inbreeding is wrong, that it will work against the laws of nature, etc. This is true to a certain extent yet authorities on pigeon and poultry breeding agree that inbreeding is the quickest and surest way of establishing and making more or less permanent the ability of birds to reproduce desired characteristics from one generation to another and practically weed out those features not desired. Inbreeding results in disaster and breaks down stamina when the breeder grows careless and does not keep up the highest degree of vigor in his birds and when he uses birds which show non-desired or bad characteristics. This high degree of vigor must be kept up by carefully selecting the most vigorous specimens before mating them. Inbreeding does not necessarily mean that while it is the surest way of maintaining and improving certain desired characteristics that each and every youngster will inherit these good points because they all do not and it is therefore imperative to select only the very best in every way. Therefore we see that the most careful selection is necessary and must go hand in hand with inbreeding.

LINE BREEDING

Line breeding, as it is generally understood, is the mating together of a pair of birds (closely or distantly related) and then breeding back on them their progeny or offspring. We see, therefore, that line breeding is inbreeding and by so inbreeding the progeny from the above pair we have a certain portion of the blood of the original birds flowing in the veins of the progeny. To line breed we must go about it systematically and follow some definite plan of breeding.

Line breeding should be used by all breeders if they ever hope to accomplish very much for themselves with their birds. In order to assist the readers of this book and give them a more definite idea of line breeding a line breeding chart, drawn up by the author, is published herewith.

ANALYSIS OF LINE BREEDING CHART: In line breeding we start with one pair of birds, both of which have valuable characteristics and are prepotent. Let us suppose we have such a pair of birds in 1 and 2. The youngsters from this pair are represented in block 3 and the arrows show blood from 1 and 2 merged and flowing into 3. This constitutes the second generation and gives us young birds having ½ blood of the original male and female. When these youngsters are old enough to mate we select the best female and mate her to the original cock (block 1). The best male in block 3 is mated back to the original hen (block 2). The youngsters from these matings are represented in blocks 4 and 5, the dotted lines in the chart in every case representing the female blood and the solid lines the male blood. These youngsters in 4 and 5 are ¾ blood of the original pair, those in 4 being ¾ blood of the

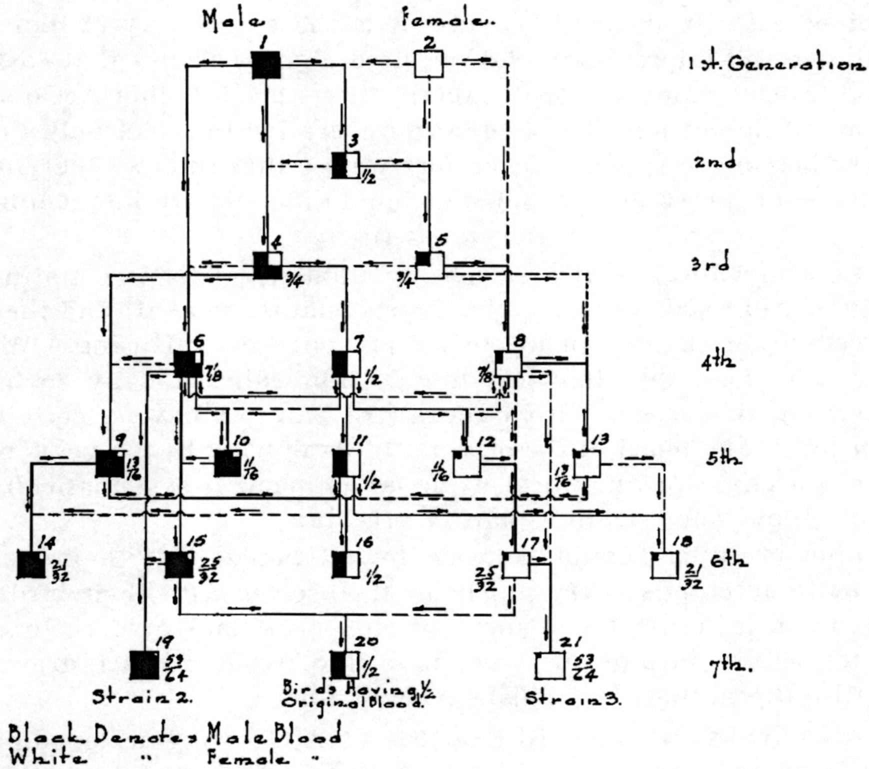

LINE BREEDING CHART.
Drawn By F. Arthur Hagard 1922.

original cock and those in 5 being ¾ blood of the original hen. Here again we select the best young hen and cock and mate the young hen back to her grandfather and the young cock to his grandmother and we get youngsters from these matings as shown in blocks 6 and 8. These are ⅞ blood of the original pair. This fraction ⅞ is arrived at as follows. The original cock's blood represents 1 and the hen mated to him is ¾. These two added together and divided by two gives us ⅞. Thus we are more firmly establishing a strain composed mainly of the blood of the original cock and breeding out the blood of the original hen. On the other side of the chart we see that we are doing the opposite with another strain. To maintain our original ½ blood we mate a cock from 4 to a hen from 5 and we get group 7 which is ½ blood or the equivalent of group 3 in a later generation. By this time the orignal cock and hen may have to be discarded or be too old. Therefore we breed our best hen from group 6 back on to a cock from 4 and we get group 9 which gives us 13-16 blood from the original cock because the cock from 4 was ¾ of his blood and the hen from 6 was ⅞. These two fractions added together gives us 13-8 and ½ of which is 13-16. By mating a cock from 8 with a hen from 5 we get group 13 which contains 13-16 of the blood of the original hen 2. At this point we again mate to get more ½ blood birds and we do this by mating birds from 6 and 8 as shown. (Notice the line running out of the bottom of group 6 and line from group 8 meeting below 7 and running into group 11.) Now we mate a cock from 6 to a ½ blood hen from 7 and the result is group 10 which represents youngsters containing 11-16 of the blood of the original cock 1. Likewise we mate a cock from 7 back to a hen from 8 and we get group 12 which is 11-16 of the blood of the original hen 2. At this point we select a cock from our male line in group 9 and mate him to a hen from group 13, our female line, and get group 16 thus maintaining ½ bloods. Group 14 is obtained by mating a cock from group 9 to a hen from group 11, the cock in this case being 13-16 and the hen ½ or 8-16 and the resultant ½ of the sum of these two gives us 21-32 of the original blood of cock 1. On the other hand we obtain group 18 by an opposite mating on the female line using a hen out of group 13 mated on a cock out of group 11. Thus we are gradually eliminating the original cock's blood on one side and the original hen's blood on the other. By mating a hen from our group 10 to a cock from 6 we get group 15 which is 25-32 of the blood of the original cock 1 or 1/8 more of his blood than is contained in group 14. On the female line by mating as shown by lines and arrows in chart we get group 17 which is also 25-32. A cock from 15 mated to a hen from 17 maintains our group in each generation having 1/2 blood each of the original birds. Now a hen from group 15 mated to a cock from group 6 will give us group 19 which birds will have 53-64 of the original cock blood. On the female side we get group 21 which is 53-64 of the blood of the original hen 2. Here we have birds that are practically the original blood of the cock and hen with which we started and have therefore established two new strains and in 20 have the original strain. It must be remembered that whenever you make a mating in either the male or female lines you must make a similar one in the other line so that you can always get back a group containing 1/2 blood of the original pair.

In the chart the arrows show the direction of flow of the blood and the little circular lines are intended to show the straight lines not connecting but as being separate and distinct.

LINE BREEDING AS AFFECTING SQUAB PRODUCING BIRDS: No doubt some of my readers will say that the foregoing is all right as far as exhibition stock is concerned but wonder wherein it applies to birds used in commercial squab production. The answer is very easy as I see it. We must realize that whenever we find an excellent pair of birds throwing large white meated squabs and plenty of them we can use this pair of birds in producing others of their kind and in this way gradually build up a flock or strain that will be far superior to others in our lofts. We will then know the parentage of our birds and know that they are of the very best and can feel much safer as regards what our squab breeding birds can and will do for we know that they have the correct breeding behind them. We can closely approximate this by carefully culling but the chances for doing so are not as good and as certain as by line breeding several pairs of our best birds because in line breeding we are more apt to get better birds,

birds that will inherit a greater number of desired characteristics and be less liable to the ill effects of some of the principles of breeding.

OUT-CROSSING: Out-crossing is commonely known as crossing the blood of one's own strain on to the blood of that of another breeder or on to the blood of an entirely different strain, though perhaps owned by the same breeder. Out-crossing and the introduction of new blood is a very risky propostion and a breeder is taking a long chance in doing either. This will no doubt seem most reasonable when we stop to consider that we do not always know the breeding behind the blood that we are introducing and we cannot therefore foretell what effect this foreign blood will have upon that of our own line. It may cause radical and serious defects to occur and bring about a general break down of our stock and even while it may not if one has good birds which are line bred and highly prepotent why take any such chance? So many times we are led to want to purchase some big winner because of the fact that he or she is such but this bird's blood may have terrible effects on that of our own. Do not do it. Breed on in line and make an equal bird for yourself. Line breeding, rigid culling and patience will enable you to do so.

CHAPTER XII

SELF-FEEDERS

Advantages of Self-Feeders—Disadvantages of Open Trough Feeding.

In other chapters I have strongly advised against the practice of feeding pigeons on the ground of the fly and on the floor of the loft. The foremost reason is that the grain will become fouled and fouled grain will cause sickness. The same thing may be said of the open trough. I have found from experience that the hopper method (Self-feeder) is not only the most sanitary one but by far the most advantageous in several respects.

We all know that birds that are setting will not always leave the nest when feed is given to the other birds. They, therefore, have to eat whatever is left over. This is indeed hard on the birds and will surely not do any good towards maintaining their bodily strength. The self-feeder should be used to offset the possibility of any bird being underfed for no matter at what time a bird may want to eat it will find grain in the feeder.

A properly designed feeder will keep grain absolutely clean. On the other hand, have you not ever noticed the filth deposited by the birds in an open trough? Can any serious minded breeder overlook the fact that pigeons do not relish grain covered with excreta from the other birds? One will surely have disease in his lofts in several forms if he is lax in the manner in which his birds are fed. It is to the advantage of the breeder to keep his breeding stock in first class condition but he can never hope to do this if he feeds fouled grain or does not take the proper precaution to keep it from becoming fouled. The self-feeder is the proper solution.

The self-feeder also cuts down the waste of feed in that it prohibits the birds from scattering the grain in every direction in their desire to first eat the choicest morsels such as peas and hemp. It is surprising to see what an amount of grain will be saved in the course of a year. Wasted grain very naturally causes a reduction in the profits of the business.

Little do some breeders realize how much time and labor is saved by using self-feeders. The properly designed feeder will hold enough grain to feed a pen of birds three days. Therefore, once in every three days we will fill the feeders whereas if we feed in an open trough twice a day we feed

SIXTEEN STALL HASCO FEEDER
Cover opened back showing grain

six times in three days or five times more than is necessary, carrying grain in a bucket or container that many times. The latter is a foolish waste of time and labor. It would be far better for the breeder to be putting in his time in some other manner, say keeping proper records.

It is a proven fact that larger squabs will be the result of using self-feeders. Why? Simply because the parent birds can eat at any time they desire and feed the squabs as many times a day as they may wish to. One will seldom find squabs squeaking for feed where self-feeders are used, showing that they are getting enough food. A careful investigation into this matter has proven this point to us beyond a doubt. The writer, formerly owner and manager of one of the largest squab plants in the Southeast, placed self-feeders in some of his pens and in others fed twice daily from open troughs. This proved to be a good test for the merits of the self-feeder and results showed conclusively that the squabs from the self-feeder pens were much larger than those from the pens in which the open troughs were used.

In feeding pigeons from open troughs there are always some birds that are pushed aside and left to go hungry. These hungry birds can never work properly. Here again we see the advantage of the self-feeder. The weaker birds may be pushed away temporarily when the stronger ones are eating but when the latter have finished there will be sufficient food left for the others.

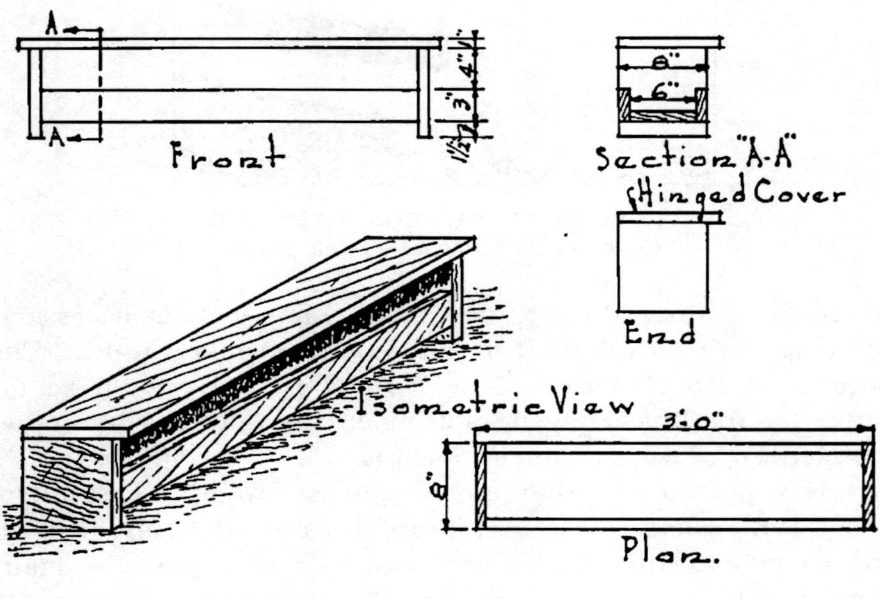

COVERED TROUGH FEEDER
Drawn By F. Arthur Hazard 1922.

CHAPTER XIII

CARING FOR THE LOFTS

Cleanliness—Whitewashing and Spraying—Repairing Lofts—Results of An Ill Kept Loft.

Pigeon lofts should be kept clean but it is indeed surprising to note how many lofts are kept in a helter-skelter fashion with absolutely no regard to cleanliness.

The wise breeder knows that he is not expected to keep his lofts absolutely spotless but he does know that he should clean up each and every loft about once every ten days or two weeks. All manure should be carefully scraped out of the spare nests, all old nests should be removed from the lofts and burned, new nesting material must be put in the crates as soon the supply therein showns signs of becoming depleted and so on. Watch the ground in the flys, don't let it get sour but turn the dirt over once in a while by spading it up and each time you do so be sure to add a top coat of clean sharp sand. Be ever on the alert to see that the health grit container has an adequate supply of grit in it and do not overlook the crushed charcoal and the necessary lump of rock salt. The fountain and the bath pans should be scalded once a week to make sure that all filth and disease germs in them are killed.

At least twice a year the entire plant, inside and out, should be given a thorough cleaning and a good thick coat of whitewash. I believe it is the U. S. Department of Agriculture that has an excellent formula for whitewash. This may be had by writing to the proper authorities in Washington for it. Spray it with a good disinfectant so as to get rid of all vermin. I have found that it is a much easier task to keep a pigeon loft free from vermin than a poultry house. Filth and vermin can cause a breeder far more trouble than we have space to mention.

Do not let your property get in bad repair but keep on the lookout for a leak in the roof, a torn piece of roofing, sagging doors, etc. The writer visited a plant in one of the neighboring states some years ago and found the owner very much discouraged and ready to give up, in fact he was just beginning to advertise his birds for sale. He was not making anything,

A LOFT OF SILVER KINGS

Note how clean everything is.—Photo from Jack M. Pun, Stockton, Calif.

his birds would not produce. We walked from pen to pen. The ground was so sour that it would have killed anything kept on it. I will venture to say that it had not been spaded in two years. Open pans were used for providing the drinking water for the birds and they were positively filthy, they showed no signs of having been scalded in months. But above all the roof in eighty per cent of the pens was leaking to such an extent that one could see daylight through it. It had rained in the lofts until the floor was covered with slick slimy manure, the whole building was cold and damp and as filthy as one could ever think of. What did I hear? Sniff, sniff, on every hand and I would have ventured a nice sum that ninety per cent of the poor birds had roup. The birds were large bone specimens for their breed, fine in type, but alas—victims of sheer carelessness on the part of the owner. Did he fail? I do not know but I do know that the last I heard of him was that he

SEVERAL WHITE KINGS IN THE LOFTS OF H. W. BARNETT
Cleanliness is evidently his byword.—Photo from H. W. Barnett, Oakland, Calif.

had disposed of his birds. This visit taught me a lesson and I pass it on to you, my reader, for there is something in it. You or I or any other man can take the finest bunch of pigeons in America and subject them to such exposure and neglect and ruin them in less than one year, yet you can take an excellent bunch of birds and make money and breed the strain up but you cannot do it by neglecting your duties around the lofts. If you are going to keep pigeons and make money from them keep them right in every way. I could tell you of other cases just as bad as the one above but space will not permit. But let me say I have never known them to spell other than one word and that word is FAILURE.

On the other hand the writer has an intimate friend, a Carneau fancier, just that,—a "fancier." He keeps his loft absolutely spotless, everything is looked after and I have never known him to have a sick bird and I have seen him produce Carneaux that would put some of our big winners to shame. He is so busy with his birds and their health and comforts that he will not advertise, nor exhibit, nor join a pigeon club but there is one thing he will do and that is keep his loft as it should be and he has been and is making a SUCCESS.

EATING THEIR MEAL

White Kings are seen eating their meal. Note their knightly posture. —Photo from F. Arthur Hazard, Augusta, Ga.

CHAPTER XIV

HOW TO TELL THE SEX OF PIGEONS

Common Rules for Same.

It is indeed a hard matter for most beginners, and, for that matter many old breeders, to distinguish the sex of a pigeon. Unlike poultry, pigeons have no real marks on the male or female that makes it easy for us to distinguish them on sight

A WHITE SWISS MONDAINE
Bred and owned by Edgar Satterthwaite, Stanton, Del.

There are several methods of telling the sex known to many breeders, any of which will prove to be more or less accurate.

One of the first methods that the writer learned was to watch the birds closely, especially while they are strutting. The bird that turns around in a complete circle is the cock bird. The hen never turns more than half a circle.

As a rule the cock bird has a larger and thicker neck than the hen, his general appearance is usually more masculine in most details but it takes a keen eye to pick these details out. On the other hand we find hens that have large heads and necks and which are liable to make us believe that they are of the male sex.

Take a bird up and put the fingers sidewise between the vent bones. If the bones are well separated the bird is a hen, if close together the bird is a cock. This applies to old hens only for a hen that has not yet laid her first egg will have close vent bones. By vent bones are meant the two bones at the rectum.

Still another method is as follows: Hold a bird by the head with the left hand and by the feet with the right hand. Gently stretch the bird. If it is a cock the tail will drop or lay even with the body, it is a hen if the tail will go upward.

With a little experience one can easily tell the sex of pigeons by their general appearance and movements.

CHAPTER XV

CULLING

Definition—Beginners Too Anxious to Build up a Large Flock to Realize Advantages of Culling—Culling Should be Carefully Studied—Non-Producing Birds Should be Culled.

Culling is the weeding out of specimens which the breeder does not care to use and which, in his judgment, are not the proper ones to breed from.

To build up a flock of paying birds one must go slow, act wisely and not be afraid to cull. No matter what the breed nor what the variety nor how high priced a pair of birds may be they will, once in a while, throw youngsters that are not exactly what we would care to breed from. We therefore eliminate these specimens from our lofts and the best method of getting rid of them is to kill them and not to pass them on to some one else.

Some beginners are so anxious to get a large number of birds that they are apt to save every squab for a while and later mate them up. In some cases it may be well to save the squabs, at least until the beginner learns how to cull them before they leave the nest, but he should keep an ever watchful eye on the youngsters as they grow up and make up his mind at once that nothing but the very best will do and as soon as they are grown he should be ready to save only specimens which come close to standard requirements and discard all others. However, the beginner sometimes cannot realize the advantage of this system and saves every bird and soon his stock is deteriorating instead of becoming better because of the poorer specimens. Remember, we cannot expect every bird that is hatched to be a good one, the poorer ones will happen along and are usually in the majority. Two poor specimens mated together will throw youngsters having the same, and probably more, defects than the parents.

We all know the rapidity with which pigeons multiply, they do not believe in race suicide, and some of us have seen it figured out how many pairs of birds we should raise in a given time by starting with say ten pairs. This scheme is just what

A WHITE KING COCK
The result of proper selection.—Photo from Jack M. Pun, Stockton, Cal.

I have mentioned above, a desire to save every bird hatched and at the end of the year we have a bunch of birds, some good, some bad, and others not fit for anything. In short we have a flock which a wise breeder would go through and very probably cull out sixty-five per cent. In view of the fact that pigeons do multiply so rapidly we should be willing to cull and cull until it hurts because it is the only way of building up a paying flock of birds even though we do mate wisely.

The art of culling is one that should be carefully studied. Of course in culling we must, as in other branches of this business, use a great deal of discretion. Having your standard clearly in your mind and being sure of what you are doing go among your youngsters and watch every bird carefully and satisfy yourself as to whether it will or will not do to save them for breeding stock. Do not just hurry through in a slipshod manner and throw out certain ones. Study each specimen carefully and if he is to be culled, take him out, kill him and forget it. If he is worth breeding from he is worthy of careful study, if he is not worth breeding from he surely is not worth saving just to have that one more bird in the plant.

Remember the larger number of birds you have the more your feed bill will be and it certainly does not behoove any breeder to feed pigeons that cannot show a good return. Do not be content to stop with culling your youngsters but watch your breeding stock as well. If you find a pair of birds that are not producing as they should get rid of them, for as we have said before, they are not showing a good return and are therefore not profitable. By a carefully kept system of records the drones can soon be spotted and either remated and given another trial or removed from the lofts entirely.

In culling birds much can be learned from the records. If we trace each bird that we cull we can soon see what birds are throwing the culls and things can be rectified before they go too far. This system of elimination of any but the best and a search into the records will show at once a great many things about how our matings are working out. The wise breeders will study these facts carefully.

To be successful in raising breeding stock we must resort to culling for it is a method which rids us of the drones and non-desirables. The sooner the novice learns the art of culling the better off he will be. The wise breeder culls and culls closely because he realizes that it is the only method of getting the **"black sheep" out of his strain of birds.**

CHAPTER XVI

WHY SOME EGGS DO NOT HATCH

Disturbing Eggs—Non-fertility—Air Slaked Lime—Improper Feeding.

I have been asked this question on several occasions and for years have seen it discussed pro and con in the pigeon press. There are several reasons for the failure of an egg to hatch. Nature never intended that bird's eggs should be disturbed during incubation and I am convinced that the egg germ can be killed in this manner.

Of course we must appreciate the fact that one of the chief reasons for non-hatching of eggs is because of the fact that they are not fertile. Unless the germ is imparted to the egg it can, of course, never hatch for in this event nothing is in the egg to assume life. Pigeons, like humans, grow old and lose their power of reproduction and the fact that pigeons have intercourse or tread does not necessarily indicate that the egg that the hen may lay, and the laying of which is not due to this intercourse, has been made fertile by her mate. Sometimes we find a pair of birds, both in excellent health, but which never hatch a squab though the hen lays her two eggs at regular intervals. It is a good idea, in a case of this kind, to break up the mating and mate them with other birds. In many cases these same birds, when mated to others, will lay and hatch every egg that they lay. It has come under my observation that a hen will occasionally lay two eggs at intervals and hatch only one of them each time. In a case of this kind I invariably break up this mating.

I have heard the statement made that the use of air slaked lime on the floor of the pigeon loft, as a disinfectant, is the cause of many eggs not hatching because the squabs are killed in the shell. It is true that lime is an absorbent of moisture and the theory is advanced that the lime, being dusted about by the wings of the birds, falls on the eggs and absorbs the moisture from them and cements up the pores of the egg shells. We all know that the eggs are almost incessantly covered by the parent birds during incubation and that little, if any, lime could get on the eggs and if it did it would be immediately dusted off by the feathers of the birds incubating the eggs. Lime, used as a disinfectant, does not kill squabs in the shell. This is my firm belief. I do agree with others that moisture is necessary

BIRDS JUST AFTER BATHING
Photo from Jack M. Pun, Stockton, Calif.

to a good hatch and for that reason all of the breeding stock should have access to a bath as often as possible and as weather conditions permit so that either the cock or hen can get their feathers moistened and carry this moisture to the eggs in the nest.

Another reason eggs do not hatch is the lack of proper feeding. To give strength to the egg germ the parent birds must be properly nourished. Improperly balanced rations and a great deal of them will cause low vitality and this in turn causes weakened egg germs. The result is then that though the germ may assume life in the shell and grow into a squab, this squab does not have the necessary strength to peck its way out of the shell and therefore dies.

Healthy breeding stock, properly balanced rations, sanitary conditions in the loft and frequent baths for the birds should steer any breeder clear of the misfortune of getting eggs that do not hatch. This part of the business should be watched very carefully and every effort made to reduce to a minimum the amount of non-hatchable eggs, for the production of sound, healthy squabs and plenty of them, is what makes it pay.

A PEN OF EXCELLENT WHITE MALTESE
Photo from B. A. Mitchell, Orenco, Oregon.

CHAPTER XVII

PIGEON DISEASES AND THEIR REMEDIES

Symptoms of and Remedies for Canker—Going Light—Sour Crop—Colds—Roup—Loose Bowels—Feather Rot—Wing Lumps—Mud Balls.

In a well regulated, well kept loft wherein are housed healthy breeding stock there is not much excuse for disease. However, there are times when it seems that in spite of all of our system and good management, some bird will show symptoms of sickness. As a rule we find disease reduced to a minimum only in lofts that are sanitary and where they are properly constructed and where every precaution is taken to have the birds get nothing but the cleanest feed and water possible. In order to assist the novice as well as some of the older breeders I have prepared this chapter giving a few symptoms of and simple remedies for several of the most common pigeon diseases.

Canker

This is one of the most dreaded of pigeon diseases and one of the dirtiest. It is usually caused from filth, dirty drinking water and unclean grain but principally from musty and mouldy grain. The writer has noticed that in most every case where canker has ever shown up in his flock he could trace it to cracked corn which had been fed only through necessity. This disease appears in the form of cheesy growth in one side of the mouth and throat. The growth enlarges very rapidly and prohibits the bird from eating. The affected bird can be told from the fact that he is sluggish and out of sorts, his feathers being ruffled. Canker is very contagious and should be taken in hand immediately by removing the patient to other quarters,

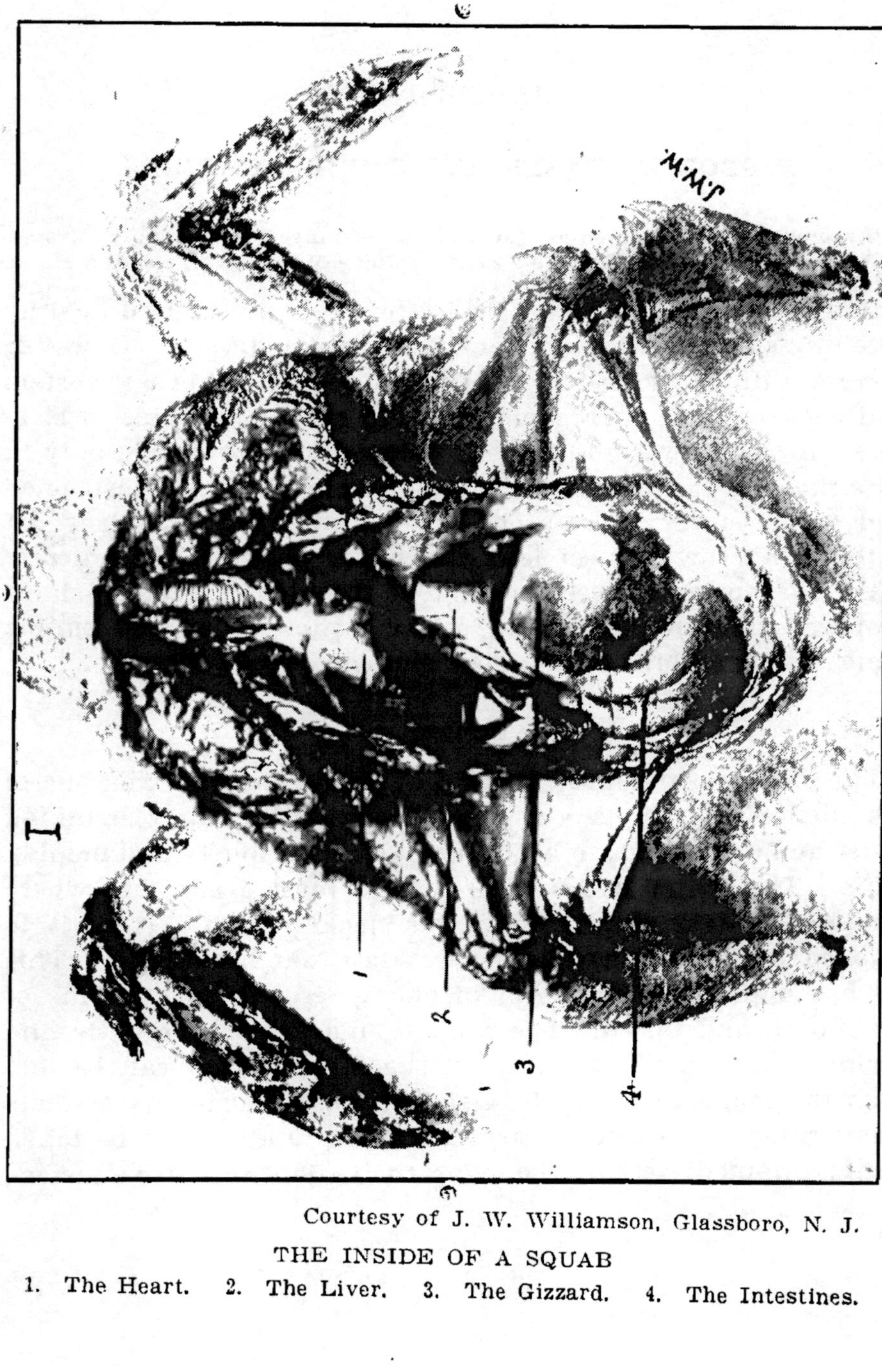

Courtesy of J. W. Williamson, Glassboro, N. J.

THE INSIDE OF A SQUAB

1. The Heart. 2. The Liver. 3. The Gizzard. 4. The Intestines.

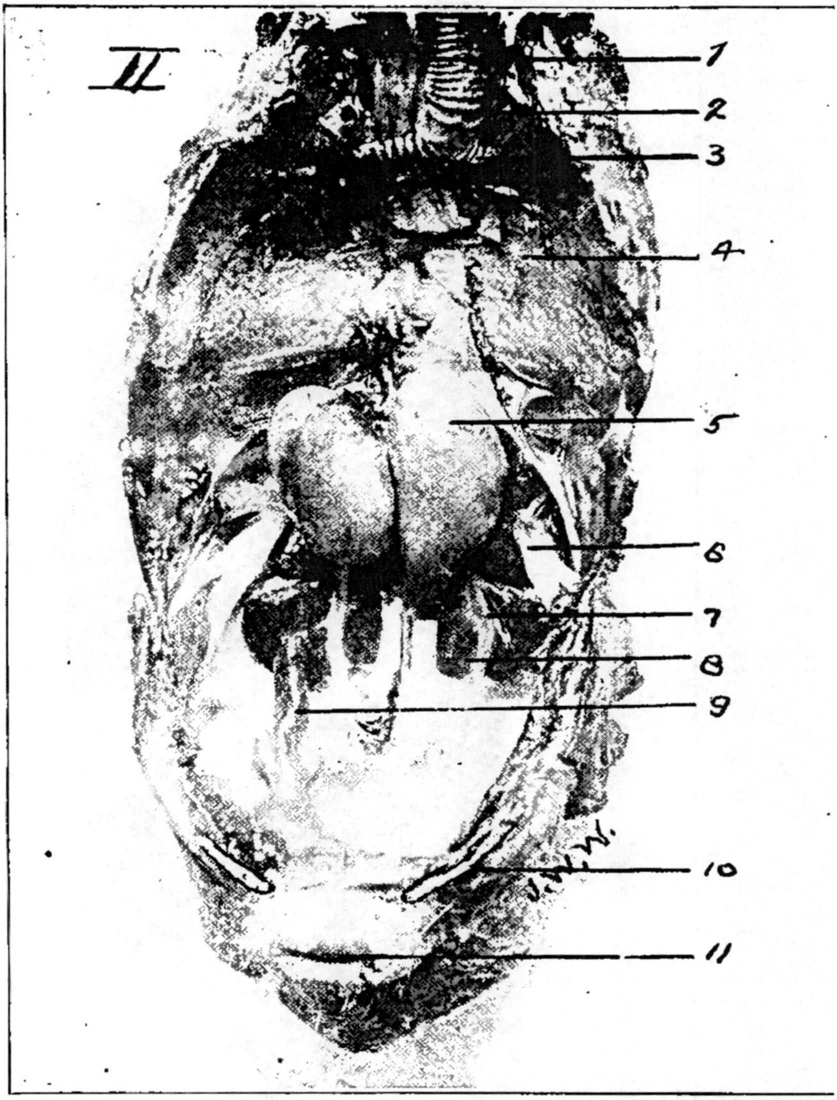

Courtesy of J. W. Williamson, Glassboro, N. J.

MALE PIGEON

1. Oesophagus
2. Trachea
3. Bronchial Tube
4. Lung
5. Testicle
6. Kidney
7. Ureter
8. Vas Deferens
9. Rectum
10. Vent Bones.
11. Anus

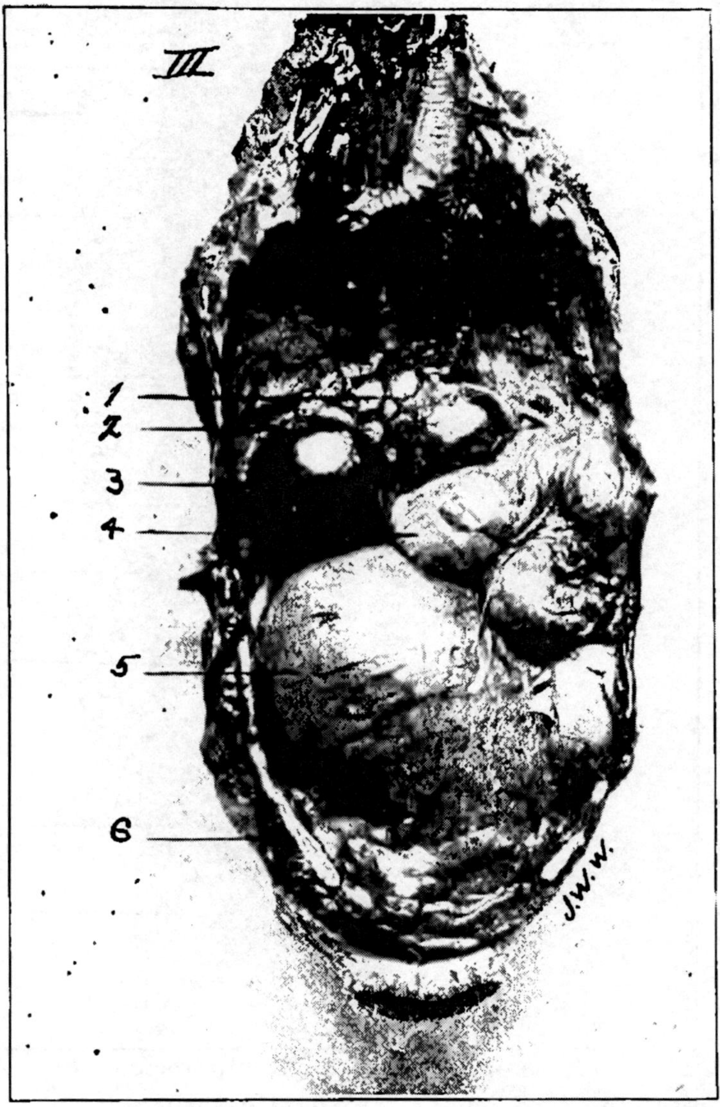

Courtesy of J. W. Williamson, Glassboro, N. J.

FEMALE PIGEON

1. Two small eggs with the ovary.
2. Two eggs a trifle smaller than the above.
3. Two that are about ready to enter the oviduct.
4. Oviduct.
5. Egg almost ready to be released.
6. Extended vent bones, showing the great distance between them compared to the male bird.

disinfecting every nook and corner of the lofts and scalding the drinking fountains, etc.

The affected bird may be treated as follows: Remove the cankerous growth with a small pointed stick and mop the raw place with a weak solution of hydrogen peroxide. After this carefully apply a pinch of burnt alum dust to the spot. Don't put in too much of this dust as the bird will inhale it causing it to choke. Place the bird in a coop by itself and do not feed until the next day or at least for eight hours. It should then be force-fed on a liberal supply of bread crumbs. As the patient shows signs of improvement place grain before it and tempt it to eat. Keep fresh water where he can get all he desires. Be sure that the bird is thoroughly cured before returning it to the lofts. If the disease cannot be checked in a reasonable length of time the best remedy is to apply the axe treatment. Remember that canker is very contagious and I believe hereditary though I must frankly admit that I have never had an occasion to check this last statement.

Going Light

This is probably the most common of all pigeons diseases. It is a wasting away of flesh and strength. It also finds its origin in mouldy grain, filthy water, etc., and from bad nourishment. An over-worked specimen that is improperly fed is an easy victim. The affected bird usually selects a secluded spot in the lofts and bunches up in a heap and, if not bothered, will remain in one spot in such a position for several hours. The excreta, or filth, issued by this bird is watery, showing the lack of nourishment as nothing is passing through the bowels.

The treatment that we have always used has been to confine the bird by itself, remove the main tail feathers one by one. Next we give a dose of about five or six drops of castor oil once a day for three days, using a medicine dropper. Force bread crumbs down the bird's throat three times a day, putting a small pinch of Pratt's Condition Powder on the bread. As the patient shows signs of improvement, and he usually will with this treatment, give ten drops of Cod Liver Oil twice a day for a few days. Tempt the bird with a few hemp seeds daily. Keep the patient in a warm (not hot) well ventilated place during the treatment. Do not allow the bird so treated to breed for several weeks after it has recovered.

Sour Crop

Sour crop is another disease which comes from filth but most often from sour, damp, or mouldy grain. Vomiting is the first symptom.

Remove the affected bird at once and allow no vomited grain to remain in the loft or fly. Several years ago the writer, being away from home on business, lost quite a few birds through the fact that his hired man accidentally fed some damaged grain out of a new shipment. An old breeder came to my rescue with this treatment. Place ten drops of carbolic acid in a gallon of water and let the birds drink same. It will invariably stop the sickness and if given to other birds will prevent the spread of the disease. This disease is contagious in this way, as we have found it. As the sick bird vomits peas and hemp especially the other birds will race to eat this sour grain and they in turn become sick. Another treatment is to give a solution of cooking soda twice a day. Care should be taken to feed only hard, dry, sound grain and this disease will rarely ever show up.

Colds

Colds are caused by dampness and exposure to drafts. The symptoms are sniffling, sneezing and rattling in the throat. Camphorated oil placed in each nostril is a good remedy. Use some of the several roup remedies that are given to poultry. A good dose of Epsom salts, say one-fourth of a teaspoonful, is another remedy as it serves to open the bowels. We human beings take a laxative for colds, therefore they should be good for colds in pigeons.

Roup

Roup is nothing more or less than a neglected cold which has grown worse. It is indeed hard to get rid of. The symptoms are violent sneezing, watery eyes and nostrils. The patient is usually feverish. Remove affected birds at once to secluded quarters as this disease is very contagious, being transmitted from one bird to another via the drinking fountain. Place the patient in dry, well ventilated and warm quarters. The U. S. Department of Agriculture recommends a very good treatment for roup in poultry in Farmer's Bulletin 957. This treatment should be a very good one for pigeons also and it would not be a bad idea for breeders to write for this bulletin. Apply to your Congressman for a copy of same.

Loose Bowels

Too much wheat is invariably the cause of loose bowels. The simplest remedy that we know of for this disease is a liberal feeding of rice. By rice we, of course, mean the hulled, uncooked rice. If taken in charge at once this disease can be cured entirely and should not give the breeder any anxiety.

Feather Rot

As the name implies this disease is a rotting of feathers. It is usually caused by the feathers being broken or bruised Remove the affected feathers and bathe the skin at the feather root with hydrogen peroxide.

Wing Lumps

One will find, from time to time, a hard lump formed on the wing butt of some of his birds. This lump is usually the result of the wing having hit against something sharp like the edge of the window or door in the loft. Again it may be the result of rough handling on the part of the breeder in that he may have dislocated the bird's wing butt while handling the bird.

It is however more usually the former. Paint the joint with Iodine daily or rub it with camphorated oil.

In some cases this lump may be more serious and prove to be a form of tuberculosis. In this case the lump will be filled with a cheesy deposit. In order to save the bird this lump should be opened with a sharp lance and this deposit removed. Mr. Vale, the noted English authority on pigeon diseases, advises that once the lump is open the deposit be removed with a stiff quill and the cavity painted with carbolized oil (one part fluid carbolic acid in nineteen parts of best olive oil) and skin drawn together with single stiches, care being taken to remove all dead skin from the wound.

Mud Balls

We have all seen pigeons with hard lumps on their feet. These lumps are caused from filth and mud being collected on the foot and they grow larger and larger until it is extremely difficult for the bird to walk. They should be removed as soon as noticed but care must be taken not to injure the bird's feet and toes. It is an excellent idea to soak the bird's feet in tepid water for a few minutes and then either cut the ball or pry it off by inserting a thin edged stick between the deposit and the top of the foot. It is not unusual for squabs to have this same trouble but they will only have it when their nest is allowed to become filthy. One will usually see that loose bowels is the cause of this trouble with squabs and therefore the breeder should start feeding rice for a few days.

CHAPTER XVIII

PREPARING SQUABS FOR MARKET

Two Markets, Private Trade and Commission Merchant—Gathering Squabs—Killing Squabs—Plucking and Washing—Shipment.

When squabs reach the age of four weeks they are fully feathered and are ready for market. As they reach this age they must be collected and killed. In order to obtain the best prices for squabs one must not be careless in preparing them for the markets. It is a proven fact that a poorly dressed specimen always fails to command a good price, therefore, it is to the advantage of the breeder to see that every squab that leaves his plant is in tip-top condition.

There are two markets to which squabs may be sold; one is to the private trade and the other to the commission men in the larger cities who annually handle thousands of squabs. For either, market squabs are killed, plucked and cooled in the same manner.

The afternoon before the squabs are to be killed we go from pen to pen and collect all that are of marketable age and carry them to the dressing room and place them in large coops over night. By collecting them at this time they will not get any feed the following morning and when we kill them we find very little feed in their crops. It is essential to remove all feed from their crops in order to have them arrive at destination in good condition.

Before killing any squabs we have a large galvanized tub filled with cool water (in the summer months we add ice). In this water is placed a heaping handful of table salt. This is done as the salt tends to make the squab meat plump and white.

When everything is in readiness several squabs are hung up by their feet on strings attached to a rack. This rack is on the wall of the dressing room and is a one inch by four inch board with six penny nails driven at intervals of four inches so that about one-half of each nail is driven in. The bird's wings are double locked so that they cannot flutter. We take a sharp narrow knife or a surgeon's lance and insert it in the

GIANT WHITE RUNT
Photo from Jack M. Pun, Stockton, Calif.

squab's mouth with the sharp edge toward the brain and with a simple twist we cut the jugular vein and the brain with one motion. This kills almost instantly. The bird is left to bleed freely for a while. Several squabs are killed in this manner and are then picked just as quickly as possible. The writer has found from experience that it is not best to let the birds hang until thoroughly cool before picking as the feathers will set more firmly and in an endeavor to remove same the picker will invariably tear the flesh. This operation is repeated until they have all been killed and picked. Never kill a great many at one time and put them in a pile. As they are picked they are thrown into the tub of water mentioned above. Each squab has its crop thoroughly washed out by forcing water down its throat. This is easily done with the aid of a stream from a garden hose nozzle. The stream can be regulated at the spigot or at the nozzle so that it will work nicely. After the crop is filled with water take the squab's head in the left hand, its feet in the right

SQUABS READY FOR THE COOK

hand and shake it up and down. If there is any feed in the crop it will become loosened by this motion and mix with the water. Let the head drop, still holding the bird by the feet. Water and grain will come out of its mouth. A couple of such operations will usually remove all grain. Next wash the bird all over carefully, removing all foreign matter, blood, filth, etc., from its feet and body. As soon as all the squabs have received their final washing we invariably pack them in ice and freeze them before shipping. This gives them a good start.

For shipment use a clean wooden box that is entirely free

from odors. These can be found at almost any grocery store. Line the box with clean newspapers or some heavy paper and allow the paper to extend above the sides of the box so that it can be folded over when the box is packed. Cover the bottom of the box with cracked ice about the size of a pigeon's egg. This layer of ice should be from three to four inches thick. On this place a layer of squabs packing them close to each other and alternating head and feet. On these place another layer of ice this time having it finely cracked so that it will fill all of the small spaces around the layer of squabs just put in. Repeat these alternate layers of ice and squabs until within about three inches of the top of the box. In this space is placed another good thick layer of ice and on top of that about two courses of paper. Just before nailing up the package place a card inside showing the name of the shipper, the number of the shipment, the date shipped and the number and weights of the squabs. All squabs should be weighed before packing. Do not be afraid of using too much ice. Remember that ice is a great deal cheaper than squab meat and moreover that the express companies will allow a reduction of twenty-five per cent on the gross weight of the package for the ice. Try to place squabs of one size in each package if possible. This may cause an extra package or two but the shipment as a whole presents a better appearance upon reaching the market, and will tend to bring better prices. New York, Chicago, Philadelphia, Boston, San Francisco, and Saint Louis, all have commission merchants who are eager to get regular shipments and who are paying good prices. The names of these firms will appear elsewhere in this book.

For private trade in the same town squabs should be dressed and delivered in pasteboard cartons, each squab carefully wrapped in tissue paper. Make the packages as attractive as possible.

For shipment to nearby towns where trains are frequent we use parcel post in the winter and ship by express in the summer months. When squabs are shipped by parcel post we wrap each one carefully in tissue paper and pack them in a heavy cardboard carton. This box is then wrapped in heavy wrapping paper and labeled "PERISHABLE." Besides the regular postage we place a Special Delivery stamp on the package and mark the package plainly three or four times "SPECIAL DELIVERY." This assures immediate delivery at destination.

CHAPTER XIX

NESTING EQUIPMENT

Orange Crates—Single Nest Systems—Double Nest System—Nest Bowls.

There are several different types of nests that can be used to advantage in the squab plant today and it is our desire to present, in this chapter, detailed working drawings of these different types in order that the beginner may be started on the correct road and also to aid the older breeder who may be contemplating remodeling his lofts.

In another chapter we told the novice that orange crates would serve the purpose for nests. They will do this but it is much better to have nests constructed on more modern lines and if he has decided to change from the old house to the new and more modern one he should by all means provide modern nests of one of the types shown herein. Orange crates, though serving the purpose well, cannot be kept in as sanitary a condition as the nests that we are showing herewith and furthermore as time goes on and the crates remain in the loft we will find mice building their nests in between the crates.

The simplest form of nests is shown in an accompanying drawing and is what is known as the Single Nest System. Each nest is made twelve inches square and twelve inches high. This will provide ample space for even large birds but in the case of Runts we believe that it would be better to make each dimension (breadth and height) fourteen inches. The sides of the nests run through continuously from top to bottom of the tier and on these sides are nailed cleats. These are one inch by one inch and nailed three times in their length. The nest bottoms are not nailed to the cleats, on which they rest, but are laid in on them and are, therefore, removable for cleaning. The bottom of any type of nests should be so constructed as it is the most sanitary and efficient method of construction. In one type of the single nest system, there is a board nailed across the front of the nests. This board is a one inch by four

A TYPE OF SINGLE NESTS COMMONLY USED
Photo from W. T. Helm, El Rio, Oxnard, Calif.

inch strip. This is done to keep the nesting material in the nest and the young squabs from falling out of the nests. However, where one uses nest bowls this strip is hardly necessary and may be omitted entirely.

Another type of single nest has both the front strip across the nests and the cleats are made so long as to carry a running board outside of and across the front of the nests. This type is the author's choice as it provides a lighting place for the birds when they go to the nest and also serves as a roosting place at night.

Several years ago the double nest system came into use and it is indeed a very good one and has steadily gained in popularity. We show herewith a working drawing for a tier of these nests containing twelve double nests. The drawings appear to be so clear that a detailed description hardly seems to be necessary for the ordinary carpenter can easily understand them and the construction is similar to the single nest

A CLOSE UP OF BIRDS IN NEST
Notice that they are very tame.—Photo from Jack M. Pun, Stockton, Cal.

system in many respects. In every modern pigeon loft there should be two nests for every pair of birds and the theory is that a pair of birds having squabs in the nest will soon build nearby and breed again. To aid them in this the double nest is used for this system, in a way, separates each two nests to themselves by means of a division on the running boards. It does much good and eliminates quite a bit of unnecessary fighting that will go on with the single nest system in use.

The drawings show all of the lumber in these nests to be one inch thick. Of course it would be much better to have these nests built of cypress boards one-half inch thick. The one inch material is rough lumber but serves the purpose all right. The thinner boards would make a much neater job. The nests should be kept up as high off the floor as possible in order to discourage building on the floor under the nests as some

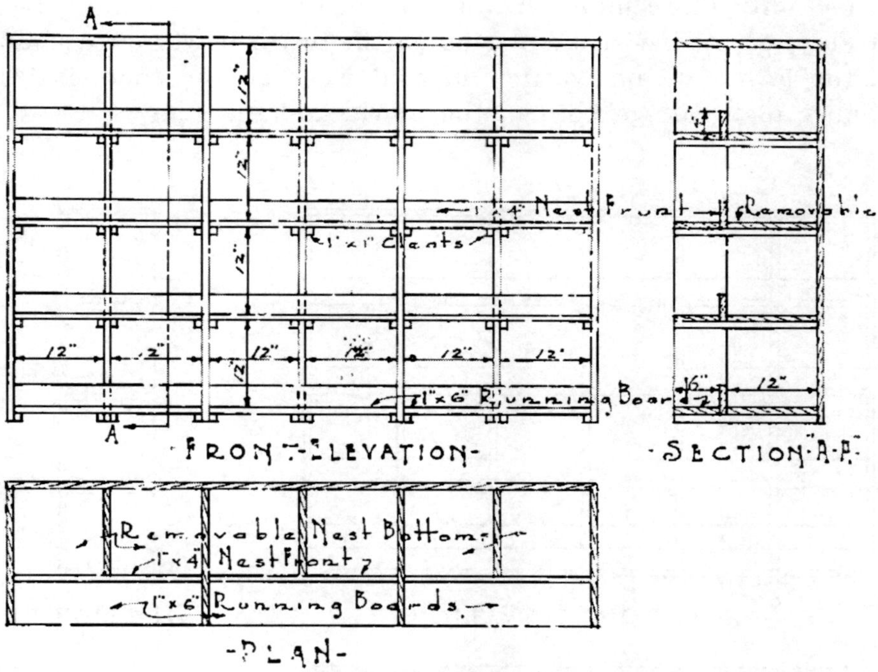

-DRAWING-FOR-A SIMPLE-DOUBLE-NEST-SYSTEM-
-Drawn-By-F. Arthur Hagard-1922. -Scale 3/4"=1'-0"-

pigeons delight in doing. On the other hand do not place the top of the nests where you cannot easily see into and reach into the top nests.

Nest bowls are very good squab house accessories and carry out the purpose for which they were designed but the writer feels that they can be dispensed with, that is that they are not absolutely necessary as some seem to think. I have raised many more hundred squabs without the aid of nest bowls than with them. The points in their favor are that they are so shaped as to provide a better home for the squabs than the square nest. If pine needles are used in a nest the poorest nest builders will have a nicely rounded nest before the squabs hatch. I would advise the breeder who wishes to install them to use only those made of fibre or pulp instead of those made of clay, or otherwise known as earthenware bowls on account of the former being warmer in cold weather and there is less chance of breakage both of the bowls and the eggs.

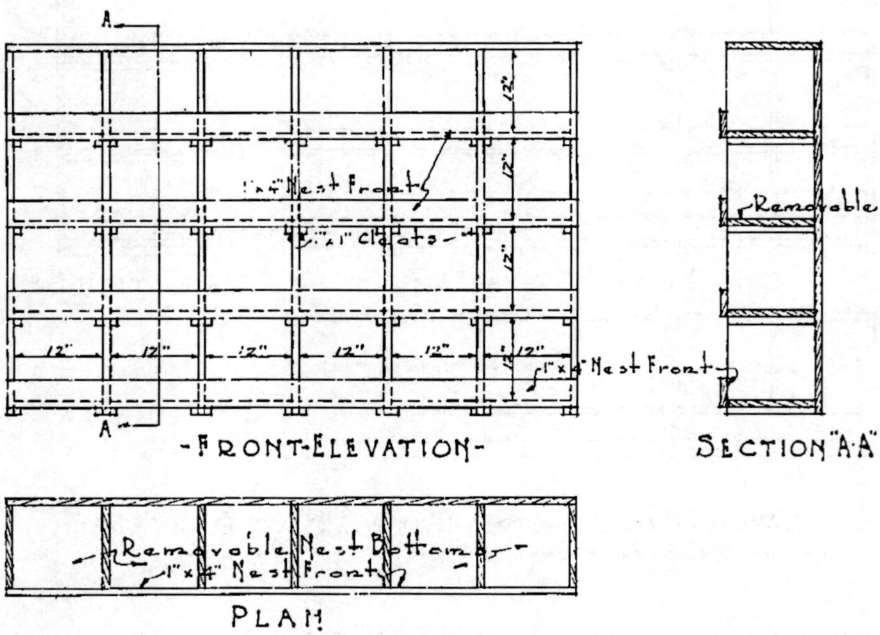

DRAWING FOR SINGLE NEST SYSTEM
Drawn By F. Arthur Hazard 1922. Scale 3/4"=1'-0"

CHAPTER XX

NESTING MATERIALS

Nesting Material Containers—Straw—Tobacco Stems—Pine Needles—Necessity of Nesting Materials.

Pigeons, unlike poultry, build their own nests. They use straw, hay, tobacco stems and pine needles to build their nests with. These materials should, therefore, be kept before the birds in the lofts at all times, in some sort of container which will keep them clean and yet allow the birds to get them with ease. Old berry crates are ideal for this purpose yet are some-

A NICE PAIR OF BLUE RUNTS
Photo from Wilson Pigeon Farm, Wilson, Kan.

times hard to get. Accompanying this chapter we are publishing a drawing showing two single nesting material racks which any one who is handy with tools can very easily construct.

Straw and hay are good for nesting material except for the fact that lice and mites find excellent homes in them. We admit that the birds like to use them on account of their light

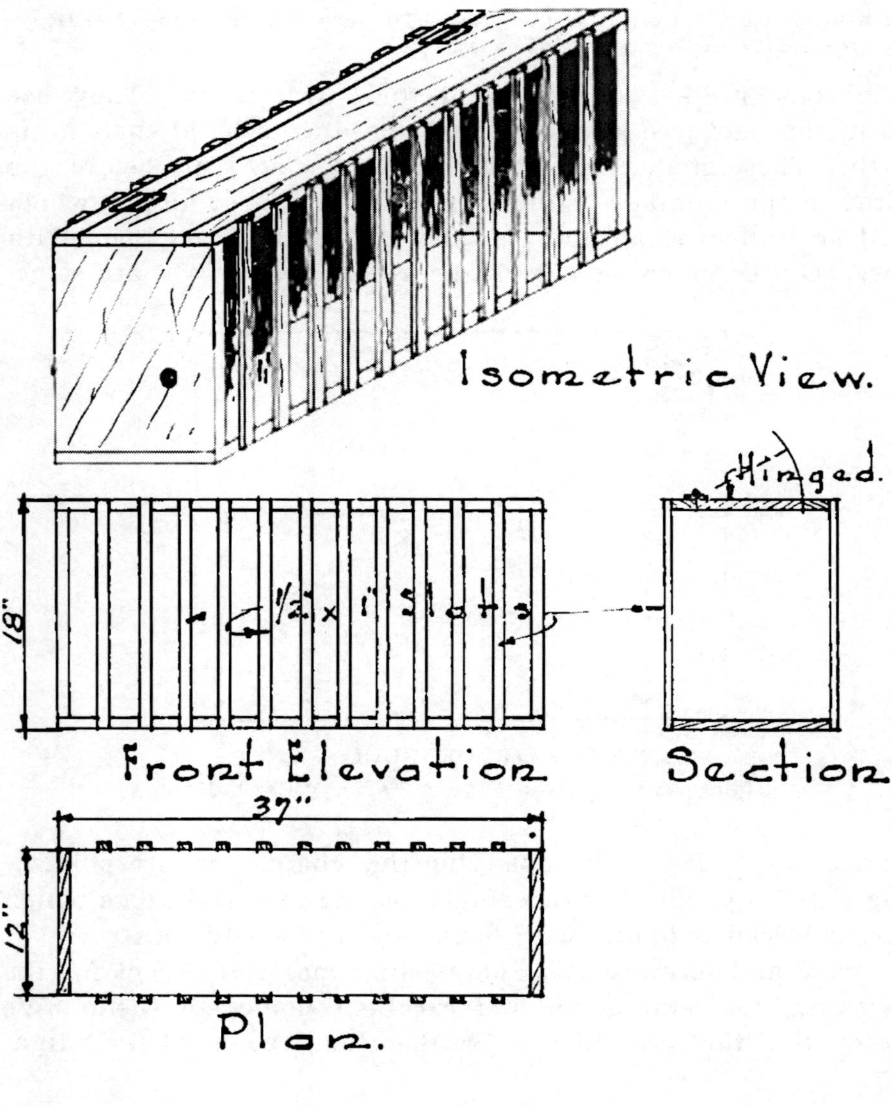

NESTING MATERIAL CRATE.
Drawn By F. Arthur Hazard 1922.

weight and the ease with which they may be handled but the writer considers them the least desirable of all the above mentioned materials.

Tobacco stems have enjoyed quite a reputation as a nesting material for pigeons. Their oder is objectionable to lice and they will drive vermin away. However, when tobacco stems

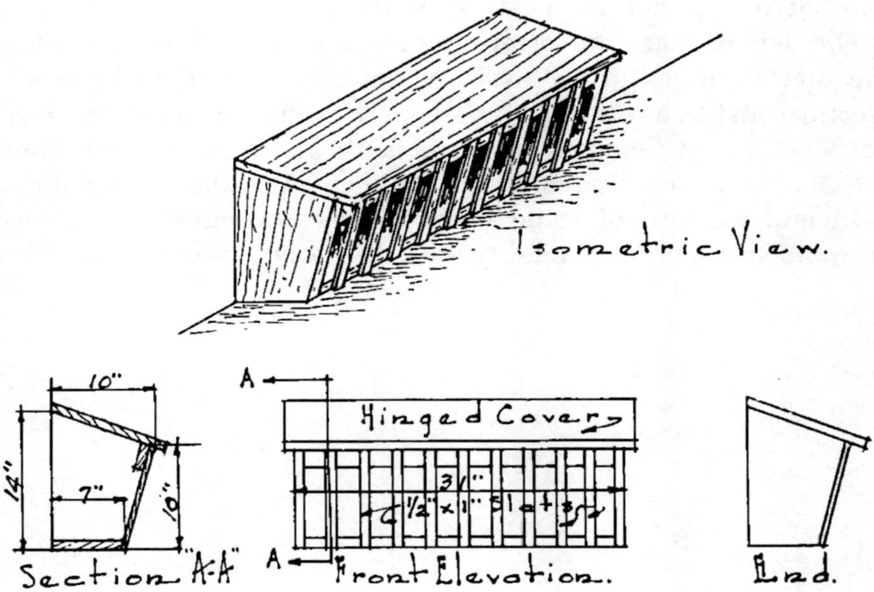

NESTING MATERIAL CRATE.
Drawn By F. Arthur Hazard 1922.

become dry they should not be used for they are more than apt to be the cause of many a broken egg. The writer has given them every fair trial but believes that wherever possible pine needles should be used instead of tobacco stems or any other nesting material. Pine needles are the leaves of pine trees and are soft and pliable and easily worked by the birds. Only dried needles should be used, those that are raked up from the ground, never those that are pulled from the trees. These needles have a resinous odor that is just as effective against lice as is the oder of tobacco stems. The writer experimented for quite a while with pine needles before advertising them and we can truthfully say that we believe them to be without a superior for nesting material.

The writer has, on several occasions, visited plants where the matter of providing nesting material seemed to be one of second consideration and the owner was crying about the birds not working. Of course the birds could not build nests without the material with which to build them. We should see that a sufficient amount of some kind of nesting material is always on hand in the lofts, a fresh supply being put in every few days.

CHAPTER XXI

SELLING SQUAB BREEDING STOCK

Raising Breeding Stock a Pleasure—Proving that Young Birds are Mated Before Selling Them—Proper Advertising Mediums—Placing Proper Prices on Breeding Birds—Properly Prepared for Shipment—Knowing How to Select Squabs to be Raised—Advertising Gained from Exhibiting—Giving Customers a Little More Than They Expect.

Some breeders do not like the idea of killing squabs but prefer to raise and mate them and then put them on the market as breeding stock. This part of the pigeon breeding business can be made to pay handsomely if properly managed and is a very pleasant part of the business.

In another chapter we have described how youngsters should be properly cared for, cooped, and raised so we will here concern ourselves, at present, only with the sale of the adult birds.

Before offering any pair of birds for sale we should always make sure from our records that they have actually produced at least two pairs of white meat squabs of the proper size. This will absolutely prove that they are mated so as to produce properly and the right kind of squabs for the market. Of course, in order to place our stock before the public we must select an advertising medium. The best one that we know of is one of the leading pigeon periodicals as in them your advertising will reach those people that are more or less directly connected with the pigeon business and are interested in what you have for sale. From time to time, as your business grows, you might place a small advertisement in the poultry magazines in the classified ad department or in the same department of the leading Sunday and daily newspapers. You will find that your advertisements in the small papers will not pay you and to advertise in them is just like throwing away money that might otherwise be well spent. In writing your advertisements make clean, clear-cut statements. Be sure that your statements are honest and offer a liberal guarantee on your birds. You can well afford to do this if you have the right kind of stock for sale and you will make friends of your customers who will later boost you every chance they get.

Place a proper price on your stock. Do not ask ten dollars a pair for birds that are worth only five and on the other hand do not offer birds worth five dollars a pair for the small sum of three dollars just to make sales. This might bring sales for a while but eventually you will brand your stock as cheap and yourself as a cheap man and the pigeon buying public will buy elsewhere for they are slowly but surely beginning to steer clear of cheap stock.

Ship only what you promise to ship; that which you have told your customer he might expect for his money. See that every bird leaves your plant in the very best condition possible, both as regards health and feather. Have them all properly banded in pairs with new open bands. All of these things count for more than you can think.

In order to properly conduct this branch of the business one must be fully prepared to carry it on. One of the first requisites which we believe goes toward making for success is the knowledge of the breeder concerning selection of squabs that are fit to raise to maturity. You cannot save just any and every squab that comes along and expect to develop them into a bird which will, when sold to another breeder, make a good name for you, to say nothing of the useless expense of raising such squabs. An old rule handed down to me and I think it an excellent one is to save for breeding purposes only such squabs as show at four weeks of age a good large frame, large feet and stocky legs and, as equally important, a broad back and a well formed breast. A squab with these qualities will invariably develop into a breeding bird that can be depended upon and one which will make his purchaser a satisfied customer of yours.

The next consideration is your equipment. You must have what is termed "Rearing Lofts" and "Test Pens." The rearing lofts are those in which the youngsters are kept until they are mated. The test pens are those in which the young mated pairs are detained and allowed to breed until we are satisfied beyond

WHITE AND SILVER KINGS EATING HEMP SEED
Photo from H. W. Barnett, Oakland, Calif.

all doubt that they are properly mated and ready to be sold or put into the breeding lofts. These lofts are arranged just the same as the breeding lofts but they should be provided in order that the birds in the real breeding lofts need not be disturbed by having young birds and newly mated pairs put in with them every few days. To do this would result in lower egg production, excessive fighting, and many broken eggs. The birds in the breeding lofts are far better off and produce more efficiently if left to themselves.

One of the best advertisements that any breeder can get, whether he is raising squab breeding stock or exhibition birds, is to patronize the pigeon shows by placing his birds on exhibition. This will result in placing your birds and your name before the public and should you be successful in winning ribbons and special prizes you will soon have a beaten path to your door for high class exhibition stock and squab breeding stock. The best squab producing birds are without a doubt, the birds that are bred closest to the standard for that particular breed and if you can win on birds that you have produced it proves that you are producing birds of the better class, birds that will prove to be really profitable as squab breeders.

Do not think that because some other breeder has made a success in selling breeding stock on a large scale that you can start where he left off and accomplish more. In any branch of the pigeon business you should start small and grow. Save only a few squabs at first and try to raise them properly. Sell them and see how you come out on it. If successful try more and more until you find that you are master of the situation. But be sure to keep advertising before the pigeon public so that you will have sales for your birds, the idea being to sell all birds as soon as you are sure that they are properly mated to secure the best results.

The surest way to succeed in this business is to give your customers just a little more than they are expecting in the way of quality of birds and quality of service. Put in an extra pair or two of birds on large orders to help offset the express charges on shipment. You will not miss them and it will more than please your customer.

CHAPTER XXII

SHIPPING BREEDING STOCK

Crude Manner of Shipping—Nest Coops Needed—Shipping Each Mated Pair in a Separate Compartment—Providing Feed—Bill of Material for Shipping Coops.

It is indeed poor policy to ship pigeons in a crude manner for we must realize that not only will the birds be subjected to careless handling en route to destination but the appearance of the crate will make either a good or bad impression on the party to whom the birds are consigned and a bad impression is certainly not what is desired. We cannot but feel sorry for the man who advises squab breeders and especially the beginners that shipping birds in any kind of a box will be all right. Doing things half way has never gotten any one very far and certainly not when he is dealing with the public.

If only a few birds are to be shipped, say one pair, a light, substantial, neat box of sufficient size will answer the purpose well, provided one end is knocked out and a slatted end substituted. On this end a small trough should be provided for feed and water cups to be fastened in. These cups should have a small board in between them of such height that will prohibit the water from splashing over on the feed. The top of the box is then slatted also. This allows plenty of fresh air to circulate through the crate and also keeps the birds from being suffocated should a careless express messenger place another package on top of the crate.

We are firm believers in crating each pair separately because of the fact that when birds are shipped in a bunch some of them will become trampled and killed through suffocation. We have prepared a drawing showing how easily an attractive and durable shipping crate can be made. Where a breeder ships many birds it will pay him to own a supply of these crates and have it thoroughly understood that the crates are to be returned when the birds are removed therefrom at destination. They are returned at a very low express rate.

A small bag of feed should be attached to the top of the shipping crate with a stout string. This bag should contain enough feed to last the birds throughout their journey and due

A PEN OF YELLOW CARNEAUX
Photo from Wilson Pigeon Farm, Wilson, Kan.

allowance should be made for delays and lay-overs. A card should be attached to the crate, in plain sight, asking that the birds be fed and watered daily at certain hours.

To ship several pairs of birds in one compartment is nothing more than cruelty and is certainly a thing that will result in many dead birds. Not only this but when many birds are shipped together matings invariably become broken and the party receiving the birds will say that you have not shipped mated pairs when in reality they may have left your plant thoroughly mated.

A little care and forethought in shipping breeding birds will go a long way toward making satisfied customers for you.

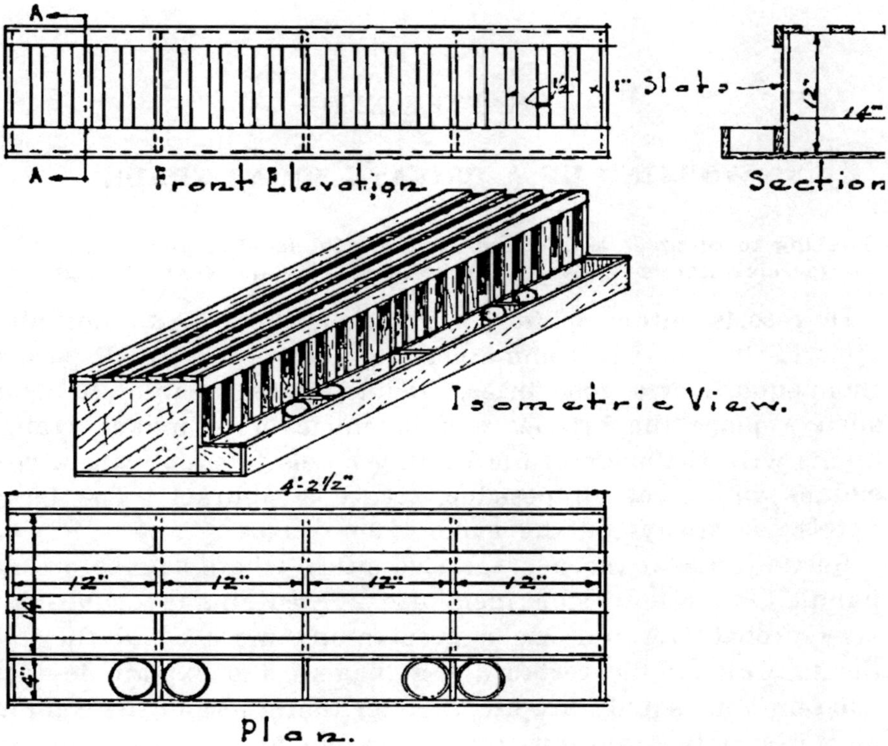

SHIPPING COOP FOR BREEDING STOCK
Drawn By F. Arthur Hazard 1922.

Bill of Material for Shipping Coops

2 pieces, ½ inch by 10 inch, 50½ inches long
5 pieces, ½ inch by 12 inches, 14 inches long.
2 pieces, ½ inch by 2½ inches, 50½ inches long
1 pieces, ½ inch by 3 inches, 50½ inches long.
2 pieces, ½ inch by 2 inches, 50½ inches long.
16 pieces, ½ inch by 1 inch, 12 inches long.
2 pieces, ½ inch by 1 inch, 50½ inches long.
4 pieces, ½ inch by ½ inch, 50½ inches long.
3 pieces. ½ inch by 2½ inches, 4 inches long.

CHAPTER XXIII

WORKING UP A PRIVATE SQUAB TRADE

Catering to Summer and Winter Resort Hotels—Restaurant and Commercial Hotels—Private Families—Making up Neat Packages.

In resorts, either winter or summer, there is an unlimited opportunity for the commercial squab breeders to dispose of their squabs at a good price. Being located near or living in such a place the breeder should endeavor to make arrangements with the chefs of the leading hotels to supply them with squabs and, if at all possible, secure a contract. The larger hotels are always on the lookout for squabs.

Restaurants in the average size cities, where squabs are not handled by commission men, use a great many squabs and very probably would use a great many more could they get them. Call on the restaurant managers and explain to them wherein your squabs are much better than those of the common pigeon variety, state how many you can furnish per week and at what price. If the proprietor does not use squabs make him a proposition to furnish him with a few if he will feature them on his menu and give them a fair trial. If you do this and he does his share you will, in all probability, make a regular customer out of him. One would be surprised at the amount of squabs that the average commercial hotels use. Go at the manager in the same manner as I have stated above in the case of the restaurant manager and no doubt you can succeed with him. Of course with this, as in other lines of selling, you will meet with a curt refusal to buy but don't give up because of that.

The author formerly sold quite a large amount of squabs to private families in the city in which he was living and in nearby towns. This is indeed a good trade for the squab breeder to cater to for having pleased one housewife she will invariably tell another or others about having purchased such nice squabs from you and in that way your private trade will grow. Look through your lofts and see how many squabs will be ready for market at a certain time and then send out neatly typewritten or printed cards stating that you will have so many squabs ready on a certain date and solicit an order. Send these cards to people whom you know can afford to pay

HUNGARIANS
Notice the graceful carriage.—Photo from Wilson Pigeon Farm, Wilson, Kan.

market prices for your product. Join the American Squab Breeders Association and get the benefit of the literature that they publish and sell to their members at cost. Distribute these booklets around among prospects and you will be surprised at the good that they will do for you.

In shipping or delivering squabs to private trade the breeder must be very particular to wrap the birds up neatly and compactly. It is surprising to know how much a neatly wrapped package counts for. See the last two paragraphs in Chapter 18 for advice concerning the preparation of squabs for private trade.

The novice or small breeder who has only a few squabs each week will do far better by selling to private trade than by trying to market his output with the commission men at some distant point because of the long haul on small shipments and greater expense in handling so few birds.

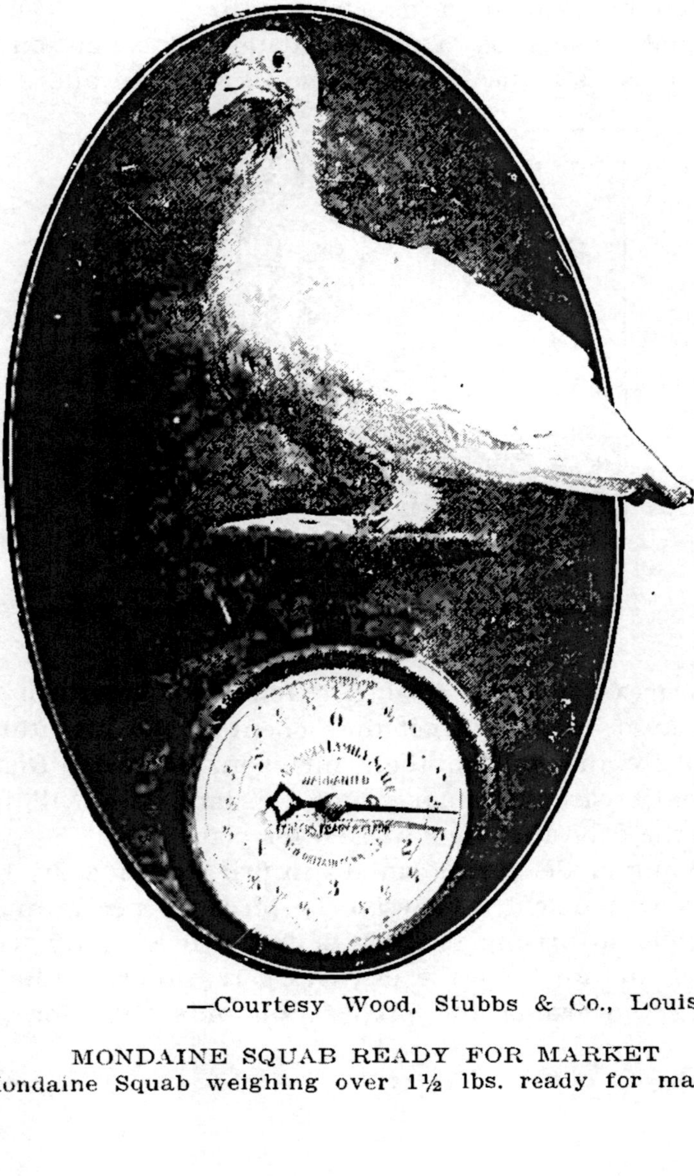

—Courtesy Wood, Stubbs & Co., Louisville, Ky.

MONDAINE SQUAB READY FOR MARKET
Mondaine Squab weighing over 1½ lbs. ready for market.

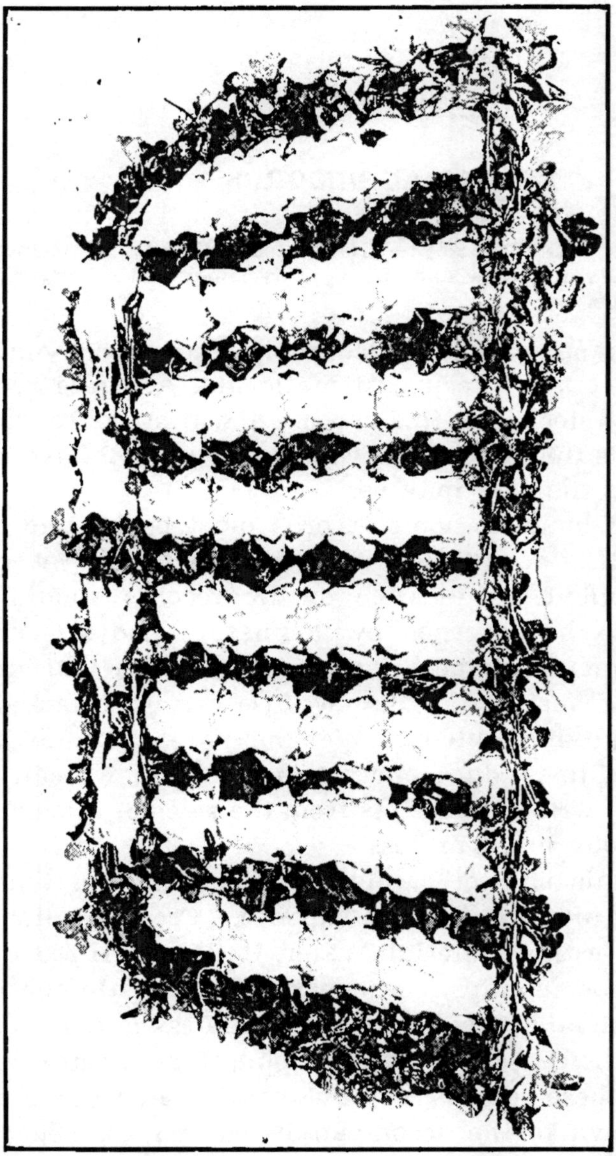

Courtesy of American Pigeon Journal, Warrenton, Mo.

AN ATTRACTIVE DISPLAY OF THREE DOZEN SQUABS

Three dozen Carneau squabs, weighing a pound each, ready for the cook. Note the neat and attractive appearance of the squabs,—a hint to those who are working up a private squab trade.

CHAPTER XXIV

FINANCIAL RECORDS

Financial Records Must be Kept—Monthly and Yearly Statements—Assets and Liabilities—Cash Book, Day Book and Ledger with Sample Entries.

In another chapter I have tried to impress upon you just how important it is to keep systematic and accurate records of your breeding stock. In this chapter I will strive to show a system of records that will prove whether or not we have made or lost money as the case may be.

In any line of business some records must be kept to show the owners whether or not they are receiving the proper return on their investment. The scope of the records should and would, of course, be governed by the nature and size of the business. Commercial pigeon breeding is not at all unlike a manufacturing business in that we use certain commodities and things to produce others. We, therefore, want to know what it costs us to produce our product so that we can then compare the cost with the receipts from the sales of this product and determine our profit or loss.

In studying this subject carefully we have found that the following enter into the cost or expense. Feed, Health Grit, Charcoal, Salt, Nesting Material, Water, Buildings, Hired Labor, and Miscellaneous (stamps, stationery, ice, etc.) On the other hand what we should receive from the business is cash for the following: Squabs, Breeding Stock, Youngsters, Feathers, Manure. To keep these records we have neatly ruled books about as we have shown in the accompanying drawings. The business records are kept month by month; that is, each month shows up for itself and at the end of the year we consolidate our twelve records into one and then we have a statement which shows us exactly what the condition of the business is at a glance—profit or loss. Not only can we become aware of how much our profit or loss is but we can arrive at the cost of feeding a pair of birds per year, and what may be expected as a return from a pair of birds, how much our hired help has cost, etc., and what part of the profits has come from the sale of squabs, what part from the sale of breeding stock, etc.

"HAPPY"—A GIANT RUNT
Bred and owned by King Lofts, Hayward, Cal. Notice the cup he won.

A great many breeders do not know whether they are making money or not. Each branch of the business should be shown up as to receipts and expenses. We can only arrive at these figures by tabulating our expenses and receipts each month. Leaks may be occurring right along and may be depriving the breeder from reaping a profit which he might justly expect but without these records we cannot discover these leaks except by accident.

When we make up our yearly statements we must always

take our breeding stock, buildings or plant and feed on hand into account and list them as an asset. Our liabilities would be whatever we owe. Of course we must charge off a fair amount for depreciation on our stock and plant. Both must be charged off yearly as both depreciate a certain amount each year. Place a fair value on your breeding birds when making up your statements—what you could actually sell them for in case you had to do so.

A PEN OF LARGE RED CARNEAUX
Photo from Wilson Pigeon Farm, Wilson, Kan.

We should keep a book known as a cash book on which we enter money received and disbursed before posting these in the as well as from whom we purchased certain items and how much we paid for each. For example. Suppose on July 15th we sell John Doe, Savannah, Ga., twelve pairs of Homers at $3.00 per pair. On our cash book on the debit side we enter the transaction thus:
ledger. The purpose of this is to show to whom we have sold squabs or breeding stock and from whom we received money

July 15th John Doe,
1422 West Harris Street,
Savannah, Ga.
12 Pairs of Homers.................... $36.00

Then, on the same date suppose that we pay the Adams Express Company $8.40 for express charges on a shipment of

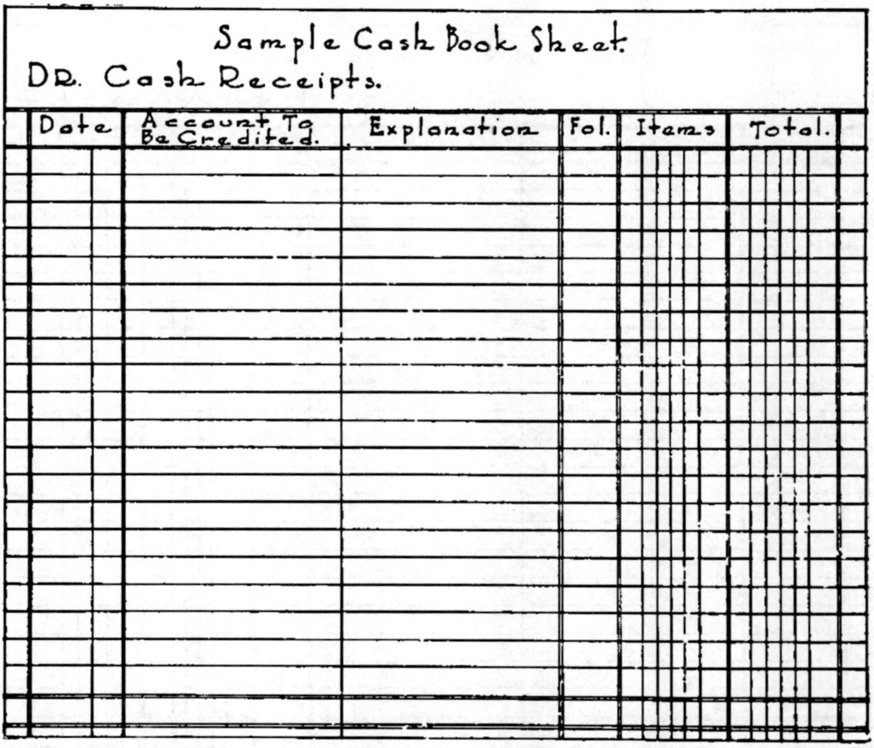

SAMPLE OF CASH BOOK SHEETS

squabs to a market in New York City. We enter this on the Credit side of the cash book, which is the right hand side, as follows:

July 15th Adams Express Company,
Expressage on shipment of squabs
to A. Silz, Inc., New York City.......... $ 8.40

In this way we have a compact record of each day's business showing clearly with whom we have had dealings and the amounts received and paid out. However, on the ledger sheets we use only figures, posting these to the ledger from the day book and each cash book leaving the notes behind as the ledger in this case is to show the disbursements for each item and the

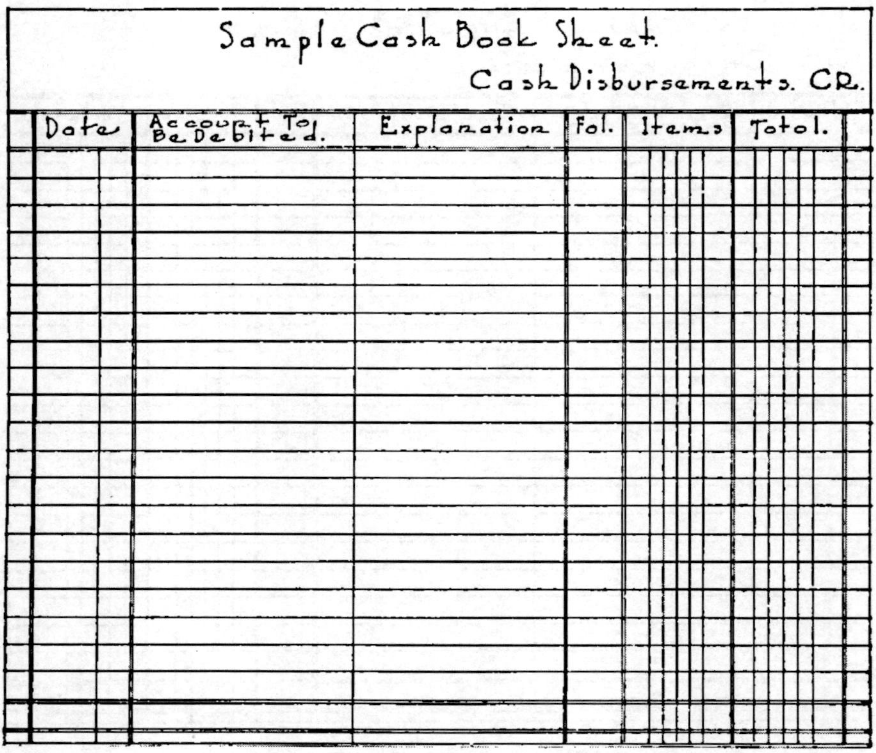

SAMPLE OF CASH BOOK SHEETS

receipts from each sale and not the names of the parties concerned.

In keeping our monthly records we simply enter each item of expense or revenue on a line by itself. The Debit side of the ledger shows the expenses while the Credit side shows the receipts. The Debits and Credits on the ledger are just the opposite from those on the Cash Book. For example. Suppose we purchase on the 18th of July breeding stock to the value of $65.00. We enter this on the disbursement side, that is the right side of the cash book and then post it to the ledger on the Debit or the left hand side for as we have just said the Debit side of the ledger shows the expense. Suppose that we purchase

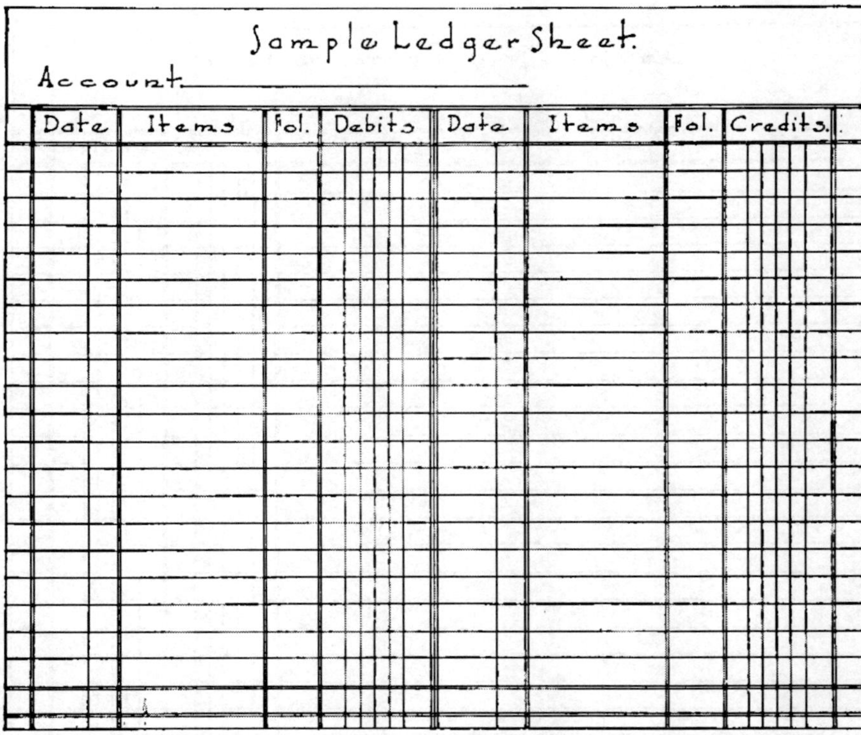

SAMPLE OF LEDGER SHEET

on the same date feed to the amount of $15.00. Likewise, on the disbursement side of the cash book we enter this item and then post it into the ledger on the debit side, putting the entries for each successive date on the line beneath the preceding one and in the proper account. On the other hand on the 19th of July suppose that we sell five dozen squabs at $10.00

per dozen. For the purpose of keeping our records more accurate we use also what is known as a day book which is nothing more or less than a Journal. If we ship these squabs to a commission merchant we must charge him with them and the day book is the proper place for the entry as there is no cash involved at the time of shipment and therefore he cannot be

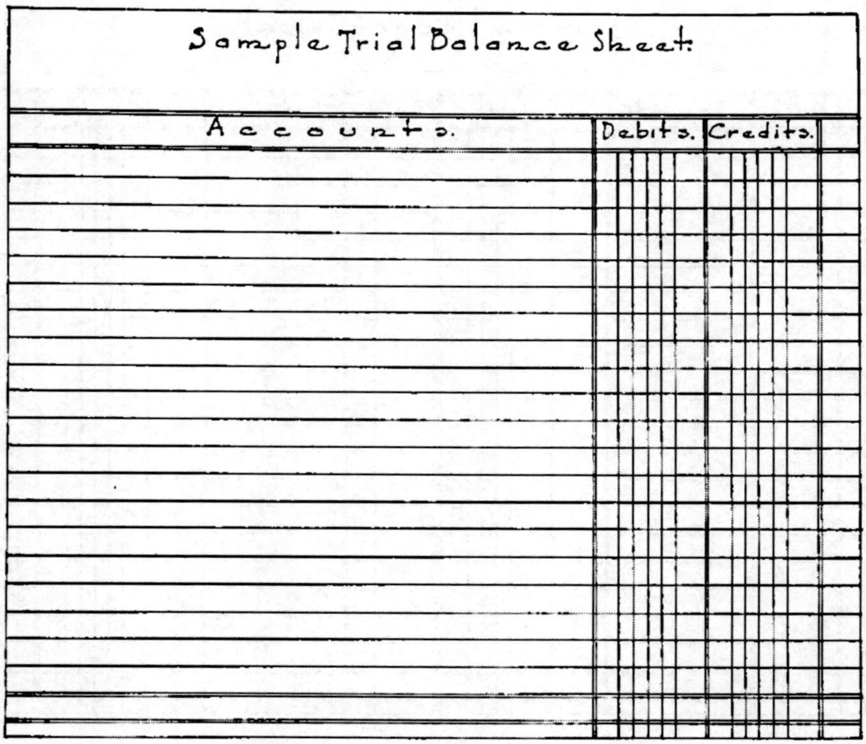

SAMPLE TRIAL BALANCE SHEET

charged with the shipment on the cash book. From the day book we post this transaction into the ledger charging the commission merchant with $50.00 and crediting the Squab Account with $50.00. On the day book our entry would show the commission merchant credited with $50.00 and the squab account debited with $50.00 as follows:

		Debits	Credits
7-19	John Doe		
	New York City		$50.00
	5 dozen Squabs	$50.00	

This applies only to accounts that are charged and when the commission merchant makes his remittance we turn to our

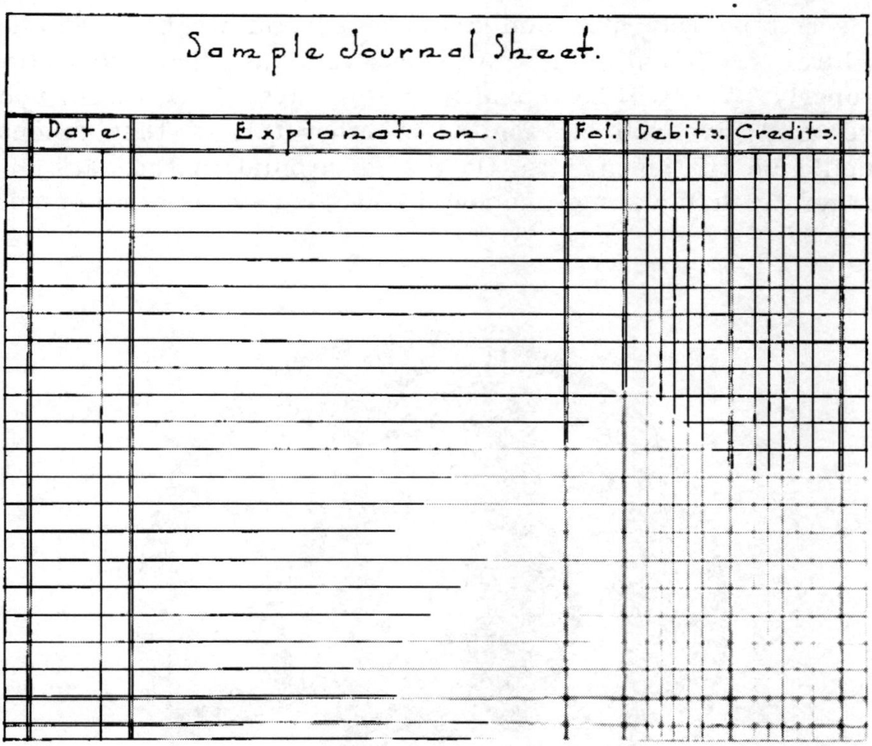

SAMPLE JOURNAL SHEET

cash book (not day book) and on the debit side of same enter this remittance which in turn is posted to the ledger on the credit side of John Doe's account and now our ledger shows his account closed.

It is in this way that we know exactly at the end of the month what our feed has cost us, what our health grit has cost us, etc., and we also know the amount received from squabs, the amount received from the breeding stock, etc., etc.

It does not take very long to make these entries and it is certainly well worth your time to keep a simple set of books. It is my firm belief that many a man has been making money on his birds when he really did not know it and being unable to see it he gets blue and discouraged and we have another failure. Try installing a set of books and enter each transaction properly. You will be repaid in many ways. It will open your eyes and give you clues as to whether this or that expense should be cut down, etc. Do not go around in the dark any longer, try to make more money by keeping systematic financial records.

SQUAB READY FOR MARKET

CHAPTER XXV

SHALL I EXHIBIT AND WHERE?

The Shows the Best Place to Learn Quality of Birds—Advertisement to be Gained by Exhibiting—Attending Shows Personally—Seeing the Judges at Work—Shows Building up Pigeon Industry—Selecting a Place to Exhibit.

The average pigeon breeder wants to exhibit his birds in competition with others in order that he may learn how his compare with the standard in the eye of a competent judge. We are all more or less eager to breed better birds than our fellow breeder; we are wanting to do just a trifle better than the other man. Of course there are some who are indifferent and who do not care. These are the ones that never get very far. By all means get the habit of exhibiting your birds at three shows, at least, each year. It is the arena in which the best are picked out and awards placed on them. It is the place where we find out who has been successful in producing birds that can win. The man who sits down in his own plant and contents himself with merely breeding birds and not showing them can never hope to make much of a success unless he is fortunate enough to have his birds win in the hands of his customers. I know of no better place for the "know all" novice to be brought to his senses than in the show room. It is there that he learns that he must work hard to produce birds that can win. It is an easy matter for a beginner to go through his plant and as he looks over his birds picture them as the best there are, but if he will exhibit them in keen competition he will soon find out and having found out he will be in a better position to size up his birds and be governed accordingly. It is to the advantage of the beginner to exhibit his birds as soon as possible.

There is indeed one great advantage in exhibiting pigeons in our leading shows looking at the matter in a commercial light. That advantage is Advertisement. There is an unlimited amount of good advertising to be obtained from exhibiting. Should you win prizes your name will be brought into the limelight; it will be written up in the pigeon press and you yourself can use paid for advertising, setting forth the fact that you have won. Breeders, and especially beginners, always want to purchase breeding stock from a man who can win prizes in keen competition. They are correct in this desire. If a man can produce birds that can win in such competition it

WHITE KINGS ON LOFT ROOF

Birds from this strain made a big win at the 1921 National Pigeon Show.—Photo from H. W. Barnett, Oakland, Calif.

proves that he is breeding his stock along the correct lines and that is just the kind of stock people want. You may sell a few birds by advertising and not showing but the minute you can advertise birds that have been exhibited and have won for you inquiries will be forthcoming from those desiring your stock. Pick up any one of the pigeon periodicals and you will see a great many of our leading breeders advertising their winnings at the largest shows. They make most of their sales on account of these winnings. If they could not and did not win they would not be listed as and considered as being among our leaders.

We should not only exhibit our birds but if possible we should attend the shows in person. In the show room many experiences are related and many good points concerning breeding, mating, culling, etc., are learned. Not only this but you are brought in touch with the most prominent breeders, you get their views on various subjects and above all you join in a good fellowship that cannot be surpassed.

There is another reason why you should, if possible, attend the shows. In a great many cases you can see the judges at

SILVER KINGS
A beautiful bird recently admitted to the King Standard.—Photo from Jack M. Pun, Stockton, Calif.

work making the awards. This should be indeed valuable to the old breeder and the novice alike. You can see for yourself why one bird wins over another and should you not be able to fathom it the judge will, if he be the right sort, tell you his reason for placing the awards as he did.

Pigeon shows go a long way toward building up the business. These shows attract a great many visitors who invariably contract a very severe case of "pigeon-fever" on the spot. Invariably this means another beginner added to our list and some one will have an opportunity of supplying breeding stock to him.

In this way many and many a breeder makes his start and each one that is added makes the industry just that much larger. It is up to you to help make the shows larger and better by exhibiting. Do not let George do it all. Help, not by wanting to, but by actually sending your birds. Pigeon shows are very essential to the welfare of the industry and to make them a success we should all help and the very best way to help is to enter your birds and, if at all possible, to be present in person.

The question of where to exhibit is rather a tedious one for us to answer because of the fact that it would not be exactly fair to mention any particular ones and exclude others. Read the pigeon magazines and see where other breeders are exhibiting their birds and be governed by that. Do not be afraid to tackle the larger ones, you may win there and if you do it may give you more ambition. If you do not win it might give you a jar that will actually be the means of waking you up and bring you to the realization that you are not producing the quality that you should. On the other hand do not play to county fair shows and think it will bring you laurels to win there. Personally, I had rather win a fifth or seventh prize at a show like Madison Square Garden or the National Pigeon Show than all the firsts at most county fairs.

CHAPTER XXVI

RODENTS AND THIEVES

Common Enemies of the Pigeon Breeder and How to Get Rid of Them.

Sparrows and mice are probably the most common enemies that the pigeon breeder has to contend with. However, with a little care and forethought these can be very easily guarded against.

If the breeder lives in a neighborhood where sparrows are plentiful he would be wise to cover his flys with one inch mesh wire instead of two inch. A sparrow cannot get through the former but he can get through the latter. Sparrows will eat quite an amount of grain out of a pigeon pen in the course of a year so they should be kept out if possible.

As a protection against mice and rats several methods may be used. We have found Stearn's Electric Paste placed on small pieces of fresh bread and put in an out of the way place in the lofts (where the birds cannot get it) will prove very effective. Of course small mouse traps may be resorted to.

The writer has, at his former home, a cat, now about six years old which he raised in his pigeon lofts and this cat never troubles a squab nor an old bird and never has done so. Many a visitor has looked surprised to see us let Tom into the pens but they very soon find out that he will not harm the squabs in any way. This cat has kept my lofts practically free from mice for the past six years and has never eaten a single squab though I have kept him locked up in the lofts at night many a time. He was placed in the lofts when a very young kitten and trained to catch mice, not squabs. It will pay breeders to own such a cat but when you try this be sure that the cat is properly fed at the house.

It is an extremely hard matter to keep rats and mice out of the lofts because the properly constructed lofts are open more or less all of the time and it is through these openings that the pests gain admittance during the night.

Experience has proven to me that it is a good idea to keep a good dog around the plant such as a Fox Terrier, Pit Bull or Airedale. A burglar confronting any one of these will usually beat a hasty retreat.

TOM—MY MOUSER

Best asset to a pigeon plant provided he is trained to catch—mice.

CHAPTER XXVII

THE ADVANTAGE OF A STANDARD

Standards Written with a Definite Aim in View—Results of Ignoring Standard—Learning and Interpreting Standards and its Reward—Advantage of Breeding Birds to a Standard—Standards a Guide for the Beginner, and Also the Breeder.

It is surprising to know how many people who enter the squab business or that of breeding pigeons forget that their breed has a standard of perfection and year after year they go on breeding their birds with but one aim in view, namely: that of producing squabs, forgetting entirely the benefits to be derived from carefully studying the standard and putting it into use.

When standards are made up by the leading breeders they are not thought out and compiled without any definite idea in view but are written with an aim toward bettering the breed both from a commercial standpoint as well as from that of exhibition. To disregard our standards and just work without any aim in view is simply wasting time and money to say nothing of hurting the breed we have chosen. To own a copy of the standard for our chosen breed and not study it carefully is nothing short of folly. The standard is a guide by which all breeders should work and by doing so better their stock in every way possible. How foolish it is to purchase good stock and allow their offspring to mate up promiscuously; to keep every bird just because it is one more in the loft when we know that a great many of these specimens do not enter the specifications of the standard. If such is allowed to go on and on we get further away from our ideal while the wise breeder is getting closer and closer to it. The time will come when our Runts or our Maltese or whatever the breed might be, will look no more like what the standard calls for than if we had not had a standard if our breeders do not use their standard as a guide.

We cannot hope to produce extra large squabs by ignoring the standard in mating our birds. Suppose our standard calls for a broad back, a deep welt rounded breast and a compact body. The unwise breeder, through his ignorance of the standard requirements, allows his birds to mate up after any fashion. small bodied birds with their like, narrow back birds with their

FRANK H. HOLLMANN (right) Editor of the American Pigeon Journal and F. ARTHUR HAZARD—Taken at Georgetown, S. C., during Mr. Hollmann's visit to the writer. Buster, a pet Fox Terrier, standing by his owner.

like and so on until finally we cannot expect to get large squabs and we do not get them. As I have said before the standards are not made only for the exhibitors of pigeons but in making them the authors have the commercial side of the matter in mind and they realize that it takes a broad back, a deep breast and a fairly compact body to produce large plump squabs, therefore they make the standards so that they will cover these points if the bird for which the standard is made is one of the breeds used for commercial squab production. The longer this non-attention to standards keeps up the poorer in grade does the offspring get. Whose fault is it that this happens? Surely the birds cannot be blamed for it.

We cannot hope to produce high grade specimens for exhibition by ignoring the standards in mating our birds. If you feel that you can do so try it for a while and then enter your birds in keen competition with those belonging to the man who has

A PEN OF WHITE KINGS
Photo from Wilson Pigeon Farm, Wilson, Kan.

worked hard and who has been guided by the standard. The chances are a great many times in his favor. He has worked for and has very probably secured what you have not worked for and have not accomplished. He has bred his birds so that they will meet the requirements of the standard and you have not. The result is that he reaps the reward and you very probably, being disappointed, blame your stock and at the same time forget that no one or anything is at fault but yourself for you have not given your birds a fair square chance.

The wise breeder will get his copy of the standard and learn it, not only almost verbatim, but he goes even further and endeavors to interpret the meaning of each part of it forming a mental picture of just what is required to make up each section of the ideal bird of his breed. When he uses this method he will have started correctly because it is the only manner in which he can know how to mate his birds or allow them to mate so as to produce the best possible results. The other wise breeder does the same thing and the only way that we can produce better birds than his is to study the standard and learn all we can and see through the meaning of the standard better than he can or does.

To the mind of the writer the breeder, who learns from the standard what is required and then strives to breed his birds to meet these requirements as best he can, is on the road to success—to produce birds that are better exhibition specimens and better squab producers than his fellow breeder—then every one will want his stock. One may not have the very best stock at the outset but if he will use a little judgment, follow the standard, and has the nerve to cull and cull till it hurts he will soon get to the top of the ladder and will meet competition anywhere and not be afraid of the results but he can do it in only one way, namely, by knowing what is required and putting into practice such breeding that will produce standard specimens and this knowledge must come from the standard for his breed.

Standards are made for a purpose and that purpose is nothing more or less than a guide for the breeder. To learn what the standard requires and then apply it is one of the most essential things in handling any breed.

I do not believe that the perfect specimen of any breed has ever been produced, at least I have never seen or heard of it. On the other hand thousands of birds are raised every year that come close to what the standard calls for and when you can breed such birds as these you can expect to make a success, not only in the show room but in the commercial plant as well. Therefore, breed to the standard.

LATEST CARNEAU IDEAL

CHAPTER XXVIII

HOMERS

Description of the Breed—The Breed Has Suffered for Lack of a Specialty Club.

The Homer is probably the best known of all pigeons as there are many more of them in use today in commercial squab production than any other breed. It is a smart, wiry type bird, being ever on the alert. They are fast breeders of squabs weighing from eight to ten pounds to the dozen dressed, though one can, by careful selection and proper mating, produce Homers that will throw squabs weighing a pound each when dressed. A great many commercial squab plants throughout this country use Homers exclusively, claiming that this breed produces more actual weight in squab meat in a year than any other breed. It is our opinion that the large Homers, those of the racing type that have been bred for size, breadth of back and depth of breast are the most profitable ones to use for squab production. Several years ago the writer was fortunate enough to secure a large number of young mated Homers of the type just referred to and these birds proved to us that it is not impossible for them to throw pound squabs.

It is indeed unfortunate for this breed that they have never had an active club to form for them a standard by which breeders could be guided. For that reason these birds have been bred in a more or less careless manner and the result has been that they have been bred smaller instead of larger. This statement of course applies to the breed as a whole but there are exceptions as some breeders have improved their birds to such an extent that they are getting pound squabs right along.

It, therefore, behooves the beginner to be careful in purchasing Homers and be sure that he is getting the larger size birds. Do not purchase Homers just because they are Homers for one will be disappointed with the small size birds, therefore demand the larger.

The writer, several years ago, owned a large plant of Homers,

RACING HOMER ON EGGS
Photo from U. S. Navy Pigeon Service.

one of the largest in the state of South Carolina, and he found them to be excellent breeders. It is true that once in a while they threw dark meat squabs but they were few and far between and if the novice likes the Homer and will get the correct stock he will not regret it.

This breed is found in practically every color in which pigeons are bred, such as white, black, blue barred, blue checker, red checker, dun, splashed, etc. They are very pretty birds and a large number of them makes a very impressive sight.

My advice to the man who owns Homers is to cull closely and wisely. By careful selection he can soon build up a strain of the larger size birds.

AN EXCELLENT WHITE KING COCK

Notice superb type.—Photo from Jack M. Pun, Stockton, Calif.

CHAPTER XXIX

KINGS

White Kings, Description and Origin—Excellent Squab Producers—Ideal Exhibition Birds—Silver Kings, Description and Origin.

WHITE KINGS: The White King is a bird of American origin. Several breeders have claimed the credit of having originated this breed but authorities have not so far been able to establish with any degree of certainty to whom the credit belongs. A Mr. Harry Troth is claimed by some to have been the originator while others state that a Mr. Harry Baker, of Elmer, N. J., is the man who gave us this grand breed. It is said, also, that the White King was produced by blending the blood of the White Swiss Mondaine, the Duchess, the Florentine and the Pouter and some say the Dragoon. How true may be the facts concerning the originator and the blood blended I am not in a position to say but what pleases the White King breeders of today most is that out of the dim past has come this beautiful snow white pigeon that is rapidly forging ahead and making for itself a remarkable record and reputation as a most profitable squab producer and an ideal exhibition bird. Several years ago the most prominent White King breeders assembled together and formed an association for the advancement of the interests of this breed. This association was originally known as the American White King Association but at the annual meeting held at Oakland, California, in January 1921, the Silver King was admitted to the standard and the association's name was changed to the American King Club and a new standard adopted.

The White King is a medium size bird, just the size to be a

fast producer—not too large nor too small. It is a compactly built bird having a body of medium length with very graceful lines that are most pleasing to the eye.

The head that is desired by the present standard is moderately large, with round skull and prominent forehead. Several years ago this was an indeed hard section for the breeders to secure good results on, the tendency of the breed being to throw offspring with a flattened skull. The same is more or less true today but there has been a very decided change for the better

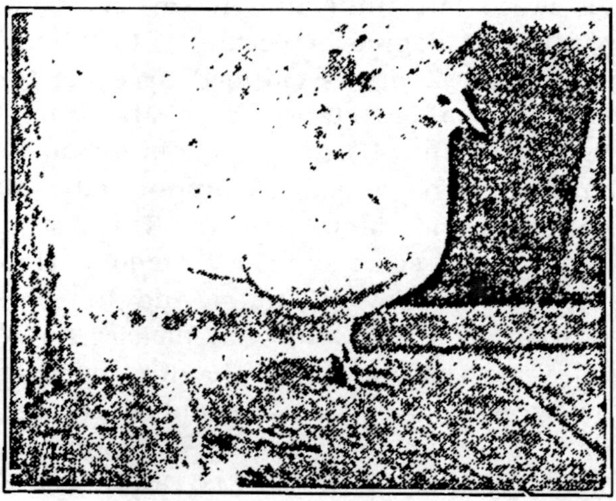

A TYPY WHITE KING
Photo from Jack M. Pun, Stockton, Calif.

in this respect. The beak, wattles and eyes of the White King are invariably nicely proportioned and when the desired rounded skull is obtained these sections make a beautiful combination. Long slender beaks should always be discarded when they appear. A stout beak of medium length is what is desired. The large rough wattle is not at all desired and care should be taken to breed for a smaller wattle of smooth texture. The prominent, keen eye is desired in the White King and should be a brownish black in color. Making for an ideal contrast we have the perfectly round eye cere which should be beet red in color. This happy combination of beet red cere and brownish black iris is indeed beautiful, set against a snow white background.

The neck of the White King should be carefully bred for and at no time should we allow ourselves to breed for bull neck specimens. It is indeed easy to do this and the author has noticed a great many Kings that have had excellent type with

SILVER KING HEN

Good type Silver King Hen, winner of 2nd prize at the 1921 National at Oakland.—Photo from Jack M. Pun, Stockton, California.

that exception. What the standard calls for is a moderately long neck, one being a happy medium between a bull neck and a long slender one, and it should blend gracefully into the broad shoulders and breast so typical of this breed.

The time is not far distant when the wings of the White King were long and their wing butts stood out and away from the shoulders but it is indeed gratifying to know that the standard now calls for a shorter wing, one that is well folded against the body and having the tips about three quarters of an inch in front of the tip of the tail. Discard birds which are habitually carrying their wings clear of the top of the tail and showing any drooped wing tendencies. Strive to breed specimens that have wing butts neatly covered by breast feathers for this makes a much better appearance from the front view.

In the back we should have one of medium length and same should be broad, just as much so as possible and this breadth

A PEN OF EXCELLENT SQUAB BREEDING KINGS
Photo from Jack M. Pun, Stockton, Calif.

should run from shoulders to tail. Try to avoid breeding from narrow back specimens if it can be helped.

A long narrow tailed specimen is not only undesirable but is very unsightly as is one which will invariably throw the tail upward. I believe this latter point is to be found mostly in the females. The tail should be rather short and by all means it should be broad. It is far better, in my opinion, to breed from a bird with a little longer tail than is desired than from one with a narrow tail. Usually a bird having a narrow tail has a narrow back and this is not desired as has been explained elsewhere in the pages of this book. The carriage of the tail is of great importance and it should always be parallel with the ground.

The breast should stand out prominently and show good width at front and sides and especially should it show well rounded lines blending gracefully into the neck and easing neatly to the lower portion of the body.

The body of this bird should be strictly on horizontal lines. The King was never intended to be a bird of vertical lines and as shape makes the breed these horizontal lines have made the King an entirely separate breed. Strictly speaking the King is a very compact bird in body and should breed very close to the standard especially in this respect. Breed for a medium length bird with broad, deep and well rounded body. Be sure that there is correct depth from back to keel and that the keel is straight.

The legs should be of medium length and straight. In color they should be bright red. No feathering on shanks and toes is allowed by the present standard and the hock feathers should round nicely at the knee and be the lowest feathers on the bird's body. Strive to overcome duck legs and by no means allow stilted legs. Both are very objectionable to say the least. Legs should be of good size and in proportion to the weight of the bird.

The White King is a close feathered bird and should be bred accordingly. A great many persons are inclined to believe the opposite, however, they are laboring under a false impression. Loose feathering is not desired at all.

This breed is an excellent squab producer of white skin squabs that will average a pound each when dressed. They are prolific breeders and our experience has been that an average pair of these birds will throw eight and nine pairs of squabs per year and it has been my pleasure to own birds that had much better records than this. They are excellent parents, being ever attentive to their young and seeing to it that they are properly fed at all times. I must say that in my experience with this breed I have found very few poor feeders. They are very easily made tame and for that reason we find very few broken eggs in the nests. Not being of a nervous disposition they care very little about any one walking around in the lofts. They are quiet and not given to continual fighting as are some of the other breeds.

The White King makes an excellent bird for exhibition purposes. They are very easy to breed and being of a solid color we do not have to worry over this point. Type is probably the main thing to breed for. The contrast of the beet red cere,

1921 WHITE KING COCK
Mr. Pun was offered $50.00 for this bird and its mate.

the red feet and shanks with the snow white plumage is all that any one could wish for.

SILVER KINGS: It is indeed good to know that the Silver King has been taken care of and now has a standard to be bred to. This standard was adopted in January 1921 by the American King Club. It is my opinion that the Silver King has a very bright future before it and indications are that it is rapidly becoming very popular. Mr. C. R. King, of the King Lofts, Hayward, Calif., is the originator of this variety and in writing in the American Pigeon Journal he explains how he made the Silver King. The following is copied from his article: "By crossing the Mondaine with the Homer and the Runt with the Maltese and then mating these two crosses together we obtained the Silver King—a short blocky silver colored bird. In choosing the different crosses I always took the bird with the silver color and discarded off colors that would crop out such as blues, etc. The Silver King has certain good qualities from each of the varieties it is made up of,—from the Homer and Mondaine, fast breeding; from the Maltese short blocky and broad breast; from the Runt, size."

The author has been very fortunate in securing several excellent photos of this new variety and they show very clearly what an attractive bird the Silver King is.

In shape or type the standard calls for the same in the Silvers as it does for the Whites. Of course coloring in the Silvers is entirely different with the exception of the wattle, cere, shanks and toes. The eye of the Silver King is pearl and the beak horn color.

The plumage of the Silver King is a beautiful silver blue leaning to a delicate fawn color and should show as little contrast as possible in shade of back, breast, wings and tail. The neck has a darker shade of fawn and with a brilliant luster. There are two sharp and well defined bars on the wings, such as is seen in the Blue and Silver Runts, and one dark bar across the tip of the tail.

In weight the White and Silver Kings should be the same.

The American King Club has its headquarters at Augusta, Ga., with F. Arthur Hazard as Secretary, and any information concerning the official standard for this breed will be gladly furnished.

CHAPTER XXX

CARNEAUX

Origin—Much Credit Due to Specialty Clubs Fostering this Breed—Principally a Utility Breed—Exhibition Bird Second to None—Description of the Different Varieties.

Different writers lay claim to the fact that the Carneau was originated in France years ago and that as far back as we can trace pigeons we find a large red pigeon, though smaller than the Runt, and which was, no doubt, the ancestor of the present day Carneau. Later we find this breed carried into Belgium and there bred for many years. It is to the Belgians that much credit must be given for the results they have obtained in perfecting this breed as a commercial squab producer. So we know very little as to who first imported this breed for several persons have claimed this credit but from several sources we learn that the first importation was made about the year nineteen hundred. Mr. A. Therrien, of West Lynn, Mass., writing in "The Carneaux" published by the International Carneau Club and Pigeon Association in nineteen hundred and ten says: "In a large consignment of fancy stock sent to me by the late Dr. M. C. Fondeur, five pairs of extra good Carneaux I found. I believe these five pairs were the first ones ever sent across the water. I have as yet been unable to find anyone to dispute this point." While we are more or less interested in knowing who made the first importation of this grand breed we are all the more interested in what the breed is and will do as a commercial squab producer and an exhibition bird. There can be no doubt in the minds of our breeders that we have perfected this breed to what it is today and much credit is due the International Carneau Club and the United Carneau Breeders Association for the excellent standard which they have provided for the breed which they foster.

The Carneau is principally a utility breed and is one of our best breeds for commercial squab production, in fact it is one of the most popular breeds of pigeons in America today. One can visit but very few small towns and not find a few pairs of Carneaux. It is a breed which can be relied upon to throw squabs weighing around a pound each when dressed. They are excellent feeders, fast workers and produce white meat squabs. It costs but very little more, if any at all, to feed Carneaux than

EXHIBITION YELLOW CARNEAU
Photo from Ned Reed, Puxico, Mo.

it does to feed smaller birds. Much has been written and said in the last few years concerning the size of Carneaux for squab production. Mr. James P. Kinnard, of Haskell, Texas, the veteran breeder of Carneaux and possibly one of the best posted men in this country on this particular breed, claims that the medium weight Carneaux are the best birds to breed from, basing his claim upon the fact that he has produced birds several ounces over the standard weights and which proved to be very unsatisfactory breeders.

The head of the Carneau should be prominent, round and gradually inclined to the nape of the neck. From the front view of the head it should be broad between the eyes and of good proportion. One thing that is fought against by Carneau breeders is a tendency toward a slender head. The skull should round gradually and show no depressions whatsoever. The eye should be large and be located a little to the front of the center line of the head on the side view. A smooth eye cere is desired and should be of nice proportions. The beak is stout and well formed, care being taken to guard against a long narrow beak which shows any stain or blackness. The wattle is smooth and V-shaped and should show no coarseness at all.

The Carneau of today is an erect, upright bird and presents

THREE GOOD TYPE RED CARNEAUX
Photos from Marion Martin, El Paso, Texas.

a beautiful carriage. The body is a solid one, compactly formed and is deep. The breast is full, well developed and should be of good proportions. The bird should show almost a straight line from back of head to tip of tail.

The neck is of good proportions and carried erect. Should be broad at junction with shoulders, forming a nice graceful line where they join.

The wings should show much strength in proportion to the body of the bird and should be carried close up and over the tail feathers, folding their tips neatly on the tail and slightly in front of the tip of same. The wing butts should fold neatly at junction with breast and not be too conspicuous. The plumage should be close-fitting in all sections.

The standard clearly sets forth the fact that the females may be more effeminate in general appearance than the males, being a little more delicate but it is especially desired that they should very closely correspond to the males in type.

SOLID REDS: The solid red variety is judged in type by the same standard as are the other varieties and differ only in color. They should have a bright, deep red chestnut color which is solid or free from off color. A faded shade of red is not at all desired by the standard. The surface color should go as deeply as possible into the fluff. The neck shows a beautiful sheen but must not be a green sheen.

SOLID YELLOWS: The solid yellow variety is judged by the same standard as are the other varieties when type is being considered. This variety is a very beautiful one with its deep golden coloring. The breeder must learn exactly what is meant by coloring and should not allow himself to breed birds showing a cinnamon color.

RED AND WHITES AND YELLOW AND WHITES: As I understand the Carneau standard these varieties are composed of those birds which cannot be judged either as Solid Reds or as Solid Yellows due to the fact that they have too many white feathers in their plumage. As a rule these are the two varieties that are mainly used in commercial squab production where Carneaux are kept because of the fact that they are not perfectly colored and therefore are not as popular for exhibition specimens.

ROSEWING REDS: Breed this variety for same type as in either the Solid Red or Solid Yellow varieties and same coloring for Solid Reds except that a few white feathers are desired in the body of the wings to form an ornamental design known as a rosette.

ROSEWING YELLOWS: Same standard applies here as for the Solid Yellows, except the wing rosette of white feathers.

WHITES: This variety is bred to the same type standard as the solid reds and is solid white in coloring. The eye should be a strong orange color and the beak either cream or white.

BLACKS: This variety is bred to the same type standard as the solid whites and is a deep raven black with a beetle green sheen. The beak is black as are the toe nails. The iris is a light orange color and the eye cere a bright coral.

The headquarters for the International Carneau Club is 144 Halsted St., East Orange, N. J., with Chanter Cornish as Secretary.

The headquarters for the United Carneau Breeders Association is 25 W. Washington St., Indianapolis, Ind., with Harry A. Stone as Secretary.

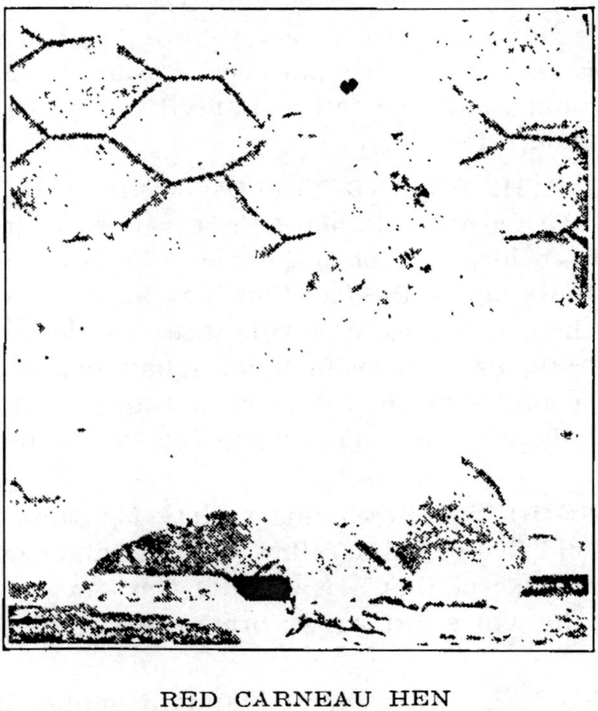

RED CARNEAU HEN

Good Type Solid Red Carneau hen, and winner of many prizes.—Bred and owned by Marion Martin, El Paso, Texas.

CHAPTER XXXI

RUNTS

Darwin on Runts—Probable Origin—Name Very Inappropriate—Runts Sometimes Bred in Individual Pens—Change for Better in Type—Runts Not Slow Breeders—Description of the Different Varieties.

Charles Darwin, the famous writer and ornithologist made quite an exhaustive study of pigeons during his life and he has handed down to us many facts that are especially valuable In writing on the history of Runts he says, in his "Animals and Plants Under Domestication:" "Of their history little can be said. In the time of Pliny the pigeons of Campania were the largest known and from this fact alone some authors assert that they were Runts. In Aldrovandi's time, in 1600, two sub-breeds existed; but one of them, the short beaked is now extinct in Europe." As far as we have been able to ascertain no one has any real knowledge as to where the first Runts came from but research reveals the fact that they were bred in many of the European countries centuries ago and our Runts of today no doubt descended from the Spanish Runt, though one of the foremost breeders of Runts in this country claims that they have come from the Roman Runt, having come to this country from Germany, and were originally known in this country as German Runts.

Why this largest of all pigeons should have been given such an inappropriate name we cannot understand for it is anything but a Runt. However, its name counts for but little for in this breed we have a bird of sterling worth and one which is steadily growing in popularity. In recent years we have noticed some of the largest breeders, and the most noted ones, take up the breeding of Runts which fact alone proves the real worth of the breed.

A great many breeders claim that Runts are best bred in individual pens while others say that they may be equally well bred in ordinary lofts containing many pairs.

Several years ago there was more or less of a tendency on the part of the Runt breeders to breed birds with drooping or dragging wings but today we notice a great change for the better, the standard calling for the wings to be well folded against the body and the tips resting on the tail. The excessive long wings are now discouraged.

GIANT RUNT

Bred and owned by Alan G. Curry, Hayward, Calif.

The upright and erect Runt with a deep, long and well rounded body and breast and a broad back, a strong beak, good stout legs and a large well curved head is indeed a beautiful bird and we find large numbers of such specimens at the leading shows today.

A great many people believe that the Runt, on account of its size, is a slow breeder. The item of size does not always enter into breeding qualities. To prove this statement let us refer to poultry and we will see Wyandottes, Plymouth Rocks and even the big Brahmas leading the small Leghorn in the egg-laying

GIANT RUNT

Bred and owned by Alan G. Curry, Hayward, Calif.

contests. It is the stock and the man handling the stock that gets the breeding results. I see no reason why Runts cannot be made to work as fast as any of the other breeds.

The head of the modern Runt should not show a flat skull nor should it be too much elevated at the highest point. It should have good size, in fact must be large and show good breadth. The back skull should be well formed and curve gracefully and gradually into the neck. The Runt being a massive bird, its head should, of course be in proportion to the size of the body. The beak should show breadth but must not be too long or narrow. In this breed we find a neat, trim, smooth wattle, small in size and it should be of a fine texture. The eyes are very prominent and well set in the center of the head looking at it from the side. The eye cere is in proportion and is fine in texture, being smooth. A rough texture on the eye cere is not at all desired and neither is a coarse wattle.

The Runt is possessed with a body of very graceful and pleasing lines. It is rather long and well formed, being of moderate depth. Great stress is laid upon the fact that this bird should have good breadth at shoulders giving it a good broad back. It is set upon well spread legs, having medium size and length shanks and toes. Taken as a whole the body proper should be as large as possible and of course the different sections should be in proportion to and fit in well with the other sections. The bird should be as close feathered as possible and its actual size should not be padded with a lot of loose feathers merely to make it appear large. Breed for a large frame and discard all loose feathered birds. The breast should be broad and full, showing sufficient depth and curving in a graceful outline from throat to keel.

The back should be long and at the same time broad and flat or nearly so. Out of the rump should come a fairly well spread tail of medium length which should be clear of the ground when the bird is standing properly.

The wings are of medium length and, of course, should be in proportion to the size of the bird's body. They should not droop nor hang down close to the ground but should be carried well up against the body with tips resting on the tail. I do not admire any Runt that carries its wings in such a position that the flights stick up above the tail and away from it. The general appearance is ruined in my opinion. How much neater and more trim the bird would be if its wing tips folded nicely on the tail. That rough appearance would then be eliminated.

In the White Runts we have a white or pinkish white beak and dark gravel eyes. These two sections in contrast with the red eye cere and pure white plumage make a beautiful sight,

PRIZE WINNING WHITE RUNTS

First bird a White Runt Cock; won first at Sacramento, 1918; first at Memphis, 1918; first and best bird in show at Knoxville, 1920; second at Hagerstown, 1920; second Kansas City, 1920. Second bird a White Runt Cock; won first at National Pigeon Show 1920. Third bird a White Runt hen; won first Los Angeles, Oakland and Sacramento, 1917; second 1920 National Pigeon Show; first Memphis 1920; second at Hagerstown, 1920.—Owned by James R. S. May, Knoxville, Tenn.

and I feel sure that the beauty of this bird has gone a long way toward making it as popular as it is today. The White Runt should be white to the skin. All type points are the same as in the other varieties.

In the Blue Runts we find a decided change from the Whites in several respects. Here we note the dark beak, in fact so dark as to incline greatly toward black. This variety has pearl eyes and damson eye ceres. In plumage coloring the ground color is a deep even shade of blue. The wings show two well defined black bars in either wing and the tail is tipped with a single black bar to match those on the wings.

The Silver Runt is a very popular variety of the Runt family and no doubt this is due to its beautiful coloring. We note in this variety a horn colored beak, pearl eyes and flesh colored eye ceres. The plumage coloring is a pale silvery blue or fawn color. The wings show two well defined dark bars across either wing and the tail is tipped with one dark bar of the same shade as the wing bars.

In the Yellow Runt we have a bird that is very pretty indeed. It is, of course, the same type as the other varieties and differs from them only in coloring. The beak is horn color, the eyes a dark gravel color, approaching black and has an orange iris. In this variety the cere is red. The surface coloring is a rich deep even shade of yellow and must be free from a faded out or mealy appearance.

The Red Runt is another very popular variety but not so much so as the White and Silver. They are no different from the other varieties in type. The plumage is a rich, deep, even shade of red throughout the surface with a red undercolor and is sound in all sections. The standard desires as little contrast as possible with the shade of neck, back, wings, and breast. This variety has a horn colored beak, dark gravel colored eyes with golden red iris, and red eye ceres.

A black pigeon, if it has proper sheen to its plumage, is indeed a beautiful sight. That is just what we find in the Black Runts for their plumage carries a nice lustrous greenish sheen. The beak is black and eyes dark gravel color with golden red iris. The eye cere is damson.

Dun Runts, as the name signifies, are dun color in all sections, the surface plumage being a dark even color. It is well for the breeder to guard against mottling or creamy color as the standard does not desire such. The beak is horn color inclining to white, the eyes dark gravel color and eye ceres flesh color.

In all varieties the shanks and toes are red.

The headquarters of the American Runt Pigeon Club is in Washington, D. C., and D. M. Green is the Secretary.

The headquarters of the National Runt Club is at Hayward, Calif., with Alan G. Curry as Secretary.

CHAPTER XXXII

HUNGARIANS

A Splendid Breed—Green on Origin of the Hungarian—Bird of Beautiful Lines—Color Contrast Great—Well Suited to Commercial Squab Production—Description of the Different Varieties.

The Hungarian is another splendid squab breeder that is rapidly making a good name for itself and we predict a very bright future for this breed. At present there are four varieties, namely, Red, Yellow, Black, and Blue Bar. I am publishing some photos of birds of this breed that will show very clearly their beautiful markings.

Mr. D. M. Green in writing of this bird, in the American Pigeon Journal, states that it came from the Florentine and was first known in Austria Hungary. The writer has never been able to ascertain to whom the credit belongs for the first importation of the Hungarian pigeon to America nor at what time this bird was first imported.

In type the Hungarian resembles the Maltese in a slight degree but the tail is not carried as erect in the former as in the latter and the legs of the Hungarian are not as long as those of the Maltese. The neat rounded skull of this bird coupled with its graceful neck, back and breast makes it indeed a bird of beautiful lines.

In color we find a decided and marked contrast in this breed for no matter what the variety it has a distinct and clear-cut white stripe, or what is commonly known to Hungarian breeders as a tape, starting at the center of the wattles and running over the crown of the head and down the back of the neck and on to other portions of the body, as set forth by the official standard, which stands out clearly and well defined against the other portions of the bird's body making a beautiful color scheme. To get this well defined tape and the proper coloring in other sections will give the breeder something to think about.

The Hungarian, besides being a bird of beautiful coloring and type, is principally a good dependable squab producer. Its broad back, deep body and well rounded breast make it an

BLACK HUNGARIAN COCK

Notice the beautiful markings.—Photo by Harry C. Weber, Hagerstown, Md.

ideal bird for such a purpose. In size this breed is practically the same as the White King. They are very hardy and vigorous and an average pair will produce from eight to ten pair of squabs per year that will weigh around a pound each when dressed—just the size that most markets prefer. The breeders throughout this country are taking to the Hungarian very rapidly and I am sure that one cannot make a mistake in using this bird for commercial squab production. Being very tame they are easily handled and we find them excellent feeders, being ever attentive to their young.

As I have done for the other breeds I will give here a sort of descriptive standard for the Hungarian though the breeder should by all means have a copy of the official standard in his possession at all times.

The head of this bird is rather a long one but sweeps in a most graceful curve from the wattle to back skull and neck making a fine appearance. It is in keeping with the size of the body and well proportioned. The eye is round, of medium size and encircled by a neat cere, the latter being of a fine texture. At the junction of the beak and the forehead we find a small neat wattle that has a fine texture. The neck of the Hungarian is rather a long one and though carried erect should not be as long as that of the Maltese. It should join the back in an easy graceful curve and be rather broad at this point.

The body of the Hungarian is what may be called "cobby," not to an extreme however to make the bird look as though it were pushed together. It should be very compact and well rounded. The standard calls for a body carried high off the ground it is not intended that this bird should have a stilted appearance. The desire to have the bird short in length of body is indeed assisted by the natural tail carriage. The tail carried at an angle close to sixty degrees and should be of sufficient length to allow the tips of the wings to rest on it when they are folded against the body. A close-feathered body is desired and this makes for a bird which presents a very solid appearance.

The breast should be carefully bred for as it is a very important section in the breed, the idea of the standard being to secure an abundance of breast meat. It should be well rounded, full and of good breadth.

The back should show good breadth from shoulders to rump, this straight portion being horizontal. At the rump there is a slight elevation where the tail springs out of same and uplifts to the angle I have previously mentioned.

As compared with other breeds having wing butts covered with breast feathers this breed differs somewhat, the idea being to gain an appearance of strength and weight by having the wing butts show clearly at front though the wings should be carried close up to the body. In keeping with the short com-

BLUE HUNGARIAN HEN
Photo from Harry C. Weber, Hagerstown, Md.

pact body we very naturally find short wings on this breed.

The legs and toes have good length and size and should never be feathered below the hock joint.

REDS: In the red variety we have a bird whose plumage shows a deep, even shade of red with the usual tape marking of white making a very beautiful contrast. This tape marking is invariably well defined. In the first part of this chapter I have explained where this tape occurs on the body of the bird. The beak is flesh color, the eyes orange and the eye cere red in this variety.

YELLOWS: The plumage is a deep even shade of yellow with the usual white tape marking. Beak is flesh color, the eyes are orange and the eye cere red. The type in all sections is the same as in the other varieties.

BLACKS: The plumage is a rich glossy black with the usual white tape marking. The eyes, beak and cere are of the same colors as in the red and yellow varieties.

BLUE BARS: The plumage is a soft even shade of blue with the usual white tape marking. On either wing we find two sharp and well defined black bars showing when wings are folded. The space between these bars is of the same shade of blue as is the remainder of the wings. There is one black bar, of the same shade as those on the wings, on the tip of the tail. The coloring of beak, eyes and eye cere is the same as in the other varieties.

All birds of this breed, no matter what the variety may be, have red toes and shanks.

The headquarters for the Hungarian Pigeon Club is at Hagerstown, Md., and Harry C. Weber is the Secretary.

CHAPTER XXXIII

WHITE SWISS MONDAINES

Natives of Switzerland—Ideal Squab Producer and an Excellent Exhibition Bird—Description of the Breed.

The White Swiss Mondaines are natives of Switzerland and as far as I have been able to ascertain no one knows definitely at what time the first importation was made nor who brought these birds to this country first.

WHITE SWISS MONDAINE HEN
First young, Madison Square Garden 1921.—Bred and owned by J. W. Geddes, Egg Harbor City, N. J.

The Mondaine is primarily a utility bird though, like the White King, Carneau, and others, it makes an ideal exhibition bird. This breed is fast becoming very popular as a commercial producer and each year finds more and more of them used for that purpose. It is rather a large bird being larger than the White King and yet not quite as large as the Runt. It is an ideal squab producing bird in that it throws squabs weighing well over a pound each when dressed and above all they are always white skin squabs. They are prolific breeders and excellent parents, being mighty good feeders. In my experience with this breed, even though it was somewhat of a short one and with only a limited number of specimens I found that while they did not give me as many squabs in a certain period of time as did some of the other utility breeds the squabs were always very much larger. They are very docile and are not

WHITE SWISS MONDAINE COCK
First young, Madison Square Garden 1921.—Bred and owned by J. W. Geddes, Egg Harbor City, N. J.

given to fighting. This breed should be even more popular than it is for certainly it is one of the best breeds that we have and no doubt has a very bright future before it. Several breeders are building up large lofts of these birds at this time and others will no doubt follow their plans.

The head of the Mondaine is of medium size and length with the eye set a little forward of the center of the head at side. A flat skull should be discarded. The beak shows strength and is of medium length and size. The eye is round and dark hazel and surrounded by a red eye cere of smooth texture. Wattles are of medium size and fine in texture.

The neck is long and carried well up and blends into the breast in a gradual graceful curve. It should be smooth and a serious objection is a short neck.

The back is long, in keeping with the general shape of the bird and tapers toward the tail but this tapering should be gradual.

The tail is long and of medium width and should be carried

WHITE SWISS MONDAINE HEN
First young, Second National Show, Oakland, Calif., 1921. Grand Champion White Swiss Mondaine Female in show.—Bred and owned by J. W. Geddes, Egg Harbor City, N. J.

well. An uplifted tail or a dragging one is a very serious defect as is also a short one.

The wings are long and carried close up to the body with the tips resting on the tail and slightly in front of the tip of same.

The breast is long in keeping with the body. An extremely broad breast is as much of a fault here as a very narrow one. Its width and depth is in keeping with the bird's build.

Legs and feet are of good size and should be free of all feathering below the hock joint. Must have good length and be set well apart and under body properly. These are pinkish white in color.

The plumage is pure white in all of its parts with a satin like luster on the neck. The fluff is pure white also.

The headquarters of the America's Swiss Mondaine Club is at El Rio, Oxnard, Calif., and Wilbur T. Helm is the Secretary. Besides this club the Mondaines have another organization working in their favor, namely, the Swiss Mondaine Pigeon Record Association of which Mr. Helm is also Secretary.

A NICE BUNCH OF WHITE SWISS MONDAINES
Bred and owned by J. W. Geddes, Egg Harbor City, N. J.

CHAPTER XXXIV

MALTESE

A Most Individual Breed — Its Make-up Well Suited to Squab Production—Principally an Exhibition Bird—Description of the Breed and Varieties.

The Maltese were imported to America not many years ago but today we find them in great numbers, especially on the Pacific Coast. To the mind of the writer it is by far the most individual bird bred in this country today. Their long legs, long slender necks and upright tails are entirely different from

A PEN OF WHITE MALTESE
Note their erect carriage.—Photo from B. A. Mitchell, Orenco, Ore.

those sections in any other breed. No doubt this individuality has gone far toward making them so popular but their real worth as excellent squab producers and ideal exhibition birds has made a very tight hold on the hearts of a great many of America's leading pigeon fanciers.

Maltese are noted for their broad, full and well rounded

breast and some claim that the breasts of these birds contain more flesh than that section of any other breed of pigeons. This fact alone would make them an ideal squab bird for in rearing and marketing squabs we all should work for the maximum of breast meat, the consumer always being desirous of securing this. They are splendid breeders and excellent feeders, producing an average of eight pairs of squabs per year and these squabs are invariably pound birds of clean white meat.

The Maltese is bred principally today for exhibition and we see some beautiful specimens at our leading shows. They

SOME DANDY MALTESE
Photo from A. F. Whelan & Son, Kansas City, Mo.

are just an ideal bird for this purpose and the breed has several men behind it who are making great strides with their birds.

We find the Maltese in the following varieties: White, Black, Red, Yellow, Blue and Silver.

The head of the Maltese is a long one, is carried high and is nicely curved from the forehead to the back skull. The cheek bones are flat and what is desired by the standard for this section seems to be an appearance of a goose head. The head on this bird is very gracefully carried and is nicely proportioned. Flatness in the curvature from the forehead to the back skull is considered a bad defect and should be guarded against. The beak is long and stout. It forms a most noticeable angle with the head in a downward direction but does not show "down-face." It differs in color with two sets of the varieties, namely: a black beak is found in Blue and Black specimens, in the others a light color beak is seen. The eyes are not prominent but are of medium size and are nicely proportioned to the head. A neat cere encircles the eye. In colors we find blue eyes on Whites, orange eyes on Blacks, Blues and Reds, and pearl eyes

A FINE MALTESE SPECIMEN

Note length of legs and neck—desired points.—Photo from A. F. Whelan & Son, Kansas City, Mo.

on Yellows, Duns, and Silvers. Whites have red ceres, Reds have flesh colored ceres, Blacks and Blues have damson colored ceres, while Yellows, Silvers and Duns have flesh colored ceres. In each case there is a nice contrast in color.

As mentioned before the Maltese have a very long, slender neck that is carried well up or erect and makes greatly for a tall bird. It is nicly proportioned. A very bad defect is a short thick neck not carried well and this should be guarded against.

The body of the bird is well rounded in almost every section and has, as stated above, a broad, full and well rounded breast carried well and slightly forward. The back is broad and short.

This broad back is indeed a very valuable asset to the breed, and comes out of a wide and well proportioned pair of shoulders. Long bodied birds are indicative of ill breeding and should not be used in the breeding pens.

The wings are carried close to the body at sides and have prominent wing butts, that is to say, the butts stand out nicely from the body to a marked degree at the front and are not

PAIR OF WHITE MALTESE
Photo from A. F. Whelan & Son, Kansas City, Mo.

covered by the breast feathers. The Maltese has short wing flights as compared with other breeds of approximately the same size.

The tail on this bird is a very short one as will be noticed from the pictures in this chapter. The tip of same is nearly square. It is carried upward. A wedge shaped tail or one that tends to droop is very objectionable.

The thighs are long and with the long legs below make this

bird a very tall one indeed. These thighs are set well apart and well in the center of the body. The feathers on the thighs are very close and present an appearance of firmness. The legs are free from feathers, stout and long. In all varieties the legs are red in color. Feet are long and well spread.

The carriage of the Maltese is very haughty and erect yet very proud and graceful. The station should be a very perpendicular one.

In coloring there are the Reds with a dark even red feather with as much luster as possible; Yellows having a nice golden

A TEN-WEEKS OLD MALTESE
Photo from A. F. Whelan & Son, Kansas City, Mo.

yellow feather with much luster, a nice rich color all over; Blues are a soft even blue with a nice green luster on the neck and a black bar on the wings and tail; Whites are a milky white with nice satin luster on hackle; Duns are a nice even dark dun color; Blacks show a lustrous black color with a nice sheen on the hackle.

A very explicit standard has been drawn up and adopted by the National Maltese Club, of which Dr. R. L. Campbell, of East St. Louis, Ill., is Secretary. Every breeder of Maltese should have a copy of same in their possession for ready reference.

CHAPTER XXXV

SQUAB MARKETS

The Commission Merchants and Their Trials—Excellent Letters from Four of America's Leading and Largest Squab Receivers.

To a great many breeders the returns from squab shipments to commission merchants are not what they might be. While Secretary of the American Squab Breeders Association it was observed by the author that the commission merchants are not always at fault for the poor returns and in a great many instances the shipper is solely to blame. There are always two sides to every question and some of us are a little too hasty to blame the other fellow entirely. It is very trying to see a shipment of nice plump squabs leave your plant and have a check come back for about one-fourth of what you expected to get. Of course shipments are delayed en route to destination and materially decrease in value and sometimes they go "green." In this case they have to be dumped and all you get is a notice to that effect signed by an official of the Board of Health of the city to which they were shipped. The commission man is up against a proposition then—he knows full well that he will be blamed wrongly. The carrier handling the shipment is mainly to blame and no doubt the shipper partially so. The carrier delays the shipment and the shipper, ten to one chances, does not properly cool the squabs before packing them for shipment. Yet the commission merchant is blamed. I have received two Board of Health dump slips from one of our largest cities and it was forwarded to me by one of the firms whose letter appears later. I then and there learned a lesson—proper cooling before shipment and plenty of ice in the container.

Under no circumstances let any squabs leave your plant until they are thoroughly frozen. If they are so treated and plenty of ice is put into the package they will go through all right and you will get proper returns.

The following letters are from four of the largest squab receivers in this country and they contain a great deal of valuable information:

June 11, 1921.

Mr. F. Arthur Hazard,
420—10th St., Augusta, Ga.

My Dear Mr. Hazard: Replying to your letter of recent date, with reference to prices of squabs, we append herewith the present schedule of prices we are paying to our shippers:

12 lb.,	$10.25 doz.	7 lb.,	$5.50 doz.
11 lb.,	9.50 doz.	6 lb.,	4.00 doz.
10 lb.,	8.25 doz.	Dark	3.00 doz.
9 lb.,	7.00 doz.	Cull	1.50 doz.
8 lb.,	5.75 doz.	Pigeons	1.50 doz.

These prices are absolutely net, delivered to us, as we do not make any deduction whatever for commission. We also make our returns very promptly, in fact, in most cases check is mailed on the same day that shipment is received.

There is absolutely no limit to the quantity that we can handle for our trade is to the very best butchers, hotels, restaurants and steamships and our outlet is such that at no time do we find ourselves with a surplus. During the season of heavy production it is necessary for us to accumulate stock to be carried over to the season of little production. Of course you will understand that the price is regulated by the demand and at certain times of the season when there is an absence of entertainments or banquets, there will be a corresponding reduction in price. During the winter months, particularly from December first to the advent of Lent, our prices are highest and we paid our shippers as much as $13.00 per dozen for the extra large squabs at one time last winter.

Squabs are of such an extremely perishable nature it is important to impress on all shippers the necessity of careful cooling before shipment and of sufficient icing. We are very happy to say that our warnings in this respect have borne fruit and it is exceptional nowadays for a shipment to reach us in bad order, due to neglect of the shipper. Of course delays of the transportation company may bring about this state of affairs, but our shippers are educated to the necessity of careful packing, icing and shipping for they realize that ice is cheaper than squabs. We are also pleased to say that some of our friends have been shipping us their squabs week in and week out for a long period, some dating back twenty years. Since pleased customers are best assets we feel that we have made good to our squab shippers.

The best days for shipping squabs are Monday, Tuesday and Wednesday. We will cheerfully answer all inquiries, and furnish shipping tags and invoice cards.

Very truly yours,

NATHAN SCHWEITZER CO., INC.

ISS—J. Isedor S. Schweitzer, Vice-President.

Mr. F. A. Hazard, May 6th, 1921.

420—10th St., Augusta, Ga.

Dear Sir: In reply to your letter of April 28th regarding Squabs, the present prices we are quoting are as follows:

12 lb., to dozen	$10.50	7 lb., to dozen	$5.75
11 lb., to dozen	9.50	6 lb., to dozen	4.00
10 lb., to dozen	8.50	Dark, per dozen	3.25
9 lb., to dozen	7.40	Cull, per dozen	1.50
8 lb., to dozen	6.25	Pigeons, per dozen	1.75

We handle from 100 to 150 dozen Squabs a day, and, while the price of Squabs must naturally be reduced to conform with the downward tendency of prices of all food products, still, there will be so many more used, that the more reasonable the prices there will be an inducement for those in the Squab raising business to increase their output to conform with the increasing demand.

After this downward revision or adjustment in prices, bringing us back to normal conditions, has taken place, the outlook then will be entirely favorable to the raising of larger quantities of Squabs for the market.

Yours very truly,

A. SILZ, INC.,

M. K. Per E. Flauraud, Vice-President.

Mr. F. Arthur Hazard, Chicago, June 8, 1921.

420—10th St., Augusta, Ga.

Dear Sir: I have been approached a good many times in the past about the future of the Squab market.

Business conditions since the first of the year have undergone a wonderful change. The people of the United States have been calling for cheaper prices on food. You have read in every newspaper, magazine, and periodical,—"Lower the price of food so we can get back to normal!"

In former years it has been the object of all the big dealers to put into the freezer the biggest part of the summer production of Squabs. I have not statistics before me, but I know that right now there is over 15,000 dozen of last year's Squabs in the coolers of Chicago. New York has a greater amount. Those Squabs were sold as a rule during the months of January, February and March in order to tide trade over during the non-productive months. I do not know about the East, but I know the slump in business struck us here in the first part of January. There were no banquets, the banks called in their loans, so consequently a big lot of broilers were thrown on the market,—and as you know, the broiling chicken is the biggest competitor the Squab has as a food.

You can buy on the Chicago market today fancy broilers at 38 cents per pound, and we are paying 62 cents per pound to the breeders, so you can see the difference in the price of the two birds. On the other hand, the greater percentage of Squabs frozen last year are still in the freezer, so none of the big operators are buying for freezing purposes. The price of feed has come down, I understand, so with the lower prices on Squabs, I still see a big future for the Squab industry, as these dark times cannot last.

I do not look for the market on Squabs to go below 50 cents per pound this year. For the months of May and June we will have paid on an average of 65 cents per pound.

It takes a long time to mate a pen of birds, and it would be a shame, after our friends, the breeders, have taken so much pains to build up the Squab industry to where it is today, to destroy their flocks, as the Squabs we are getting today are 100 per cent better than the scrawny birds we were getting years ago.

As I can remember, a year back if someone would ask me for 500 birds from 12 to 14 ounces apiece, I would not have enough birds to begin to grade that number.

Trusting that all the dealers will co-operate with the breeders, and build, and keep on building the Squab Industry to a higher pinnacle than before, and wishing them success, and hoping that the time will develop for higher prices in the near future, I remain

Sincerely yours,

AR—MC A. ROBINE.

Mr. F. Arthur Hazard, Chicago, May 10th, 1921.

420—10th St., Augusta, Ga.

Dear Friend: Your letter of the 28th at hand, and in reply wish to state that our present paying price on Squabs is 65 cents per lb., and our outlet is so large that we can use any number of them 365 days in the year.

However, the great difficulty arises in educating the breeders to properly raise the kind of Squabs that will dress out, so that they will grade a nice, big, plump bird.

Then again, there are some shippers who know very little about weighing squabs before shipping them to the market. They believe that after they have soaked the birds in water and then weighed them out in that manner, the weights should hold out at the other end. Naturally, the results are disappointing, because you know the moisture and water will soon evaporate. Furthermore, we have laws here prohibiting the selling of Squabs that are soaked in water. In other words, we have got to sell them practically dry.

Another mistake is made by shippers who will send stuff by Parcel Post, or other methods through the mail, forgetting that even though they may place Special Delivery stamps on the package the Post

Office Department has no facilities for refrigerating services. The result is a lot of decomposed Squabs.

Then again, there are shippers who do not properly ice Squabs, believing that just a little ice will carry the shipment through.

If these evils could be corrected all the shipper would have to do would be to find a place where he would receive a guaranteed price,—a house with a good reputation—and we know that this game would then be placed on a more substantial and profitable basis.

However, there are just as many receivers who need suggestions for improving the Squab Industry in general as the breeder.

For example, we spend a good many hundreds of dollars advertising Squabs,—trying to get the public to use this commodity, etc.,—while other receivers will just sell to certain clubs and hotels who will occasionally place Squabs on their bill of fare.

But what we believe would really result in a greater demand for Squabs and higher prices as well as increased profits for breeders would be a general advertising campaign, giving the public a thorough knowledge of the benefits to be derived from eating Squabs.—the same as the Grapefruit Industry, which but a very short while ago was an unknown factor.

The writer would be glad to receive a copy of your manuscript when completed.

In the meantime, if there is any further information that I can give you let me know, and I will be glad to comply with your request.

Very truly yours,

SECURITY PRODUCE, COMPANY, Inc.

SR—SM S. ROSENTHAL, President.

CHAPTER XXXVI

SPECIALTY CLUBS

Growth of Clubs Retarded by Indifference of Breeders—Practical Worth of Clubs—Conditions Under Which Specialty Clubs Labor—Duty of the Breeders to Support These Clubs.

It is indeed gratifying to note that the majority of our breeds have specialty clubs to look out for their interests. These clubs are doing wonderful work and they are growing slowly but surely. However, they are not receiving the support that they should and this lack of support is due to nothing more or less than one thing, i. e., INDIFFERENCE on the part of the breeders. There seems to be a great many men in the pigeon world who love their birds and never lose an occasion to boost them whenever a novice is around yet they never join a specialty club. If all of the breeders of Hungarians would join the specialty club for that breed think what strides that club could and would make. So it is with others clubs.

Of what practical worth is a specialty club? It is worth every bit of support that can be given it because it proves this in the things that it does and can accomplish. The breeds are boosted by these clubs, the real worth of the birds which they foster is made known in various ways and prizes are offered by them to breeders who raise the best birds of the different breeds. At all times these clubs are working toward bettering the breeds and they are doing it. Above all they make up and adopt certain standards to which we must breed our birds in order to compete for prizes, etc. It is only by breeding to these recognized standards that we can ever hope to get very far. If the specialty clubs did nothing more than to revise and better the standards each year or two they would be worth many times the small membership dues asked.

There are hundreds and hundreds of breeders who raise White Kings and yet in looking over a recent report of the Secretary of the American King Club we find only twenty-nine names on the membership directory. Why there are not more names there is due to only one thing and that is, as we have said before, INDIFFERENCE. On this club list we see the names of six men who have been members for years. These men have stuck by their breed and they have aided materially in making the White King what it is today. However, in looking over the pages of the pigeon press we find the names of men who advertise and breed White Kings and their names are not on our list.

Again we find the same conditions existing in Swiss Mondaine Clubs and others. There are hundreds and hundreds of breeders of Carneaux in America and yet the membership of the United Carneau Breeders Association does not carry the names of hundreds of members. It is certainly no fault of the specialty clubs—they are doing excellent work and are ever ready to do even more but they do not get the support that they should. These clubs would grow by leaps and bounds if the mass of breeders would join and cast aside this unwillful indifference.

No doubt a great many breeders and especially the smaller ones feel that their birds are not as good as those owned by some members of these clubs. Probably they are correct in this but if they would join and do their share they would aid the club materially and in so doing they would have set an example for others. You do not have to own the best birds in the country to become a member of any specialty club. These clubs want your support in every way and they only ask you to pay a very small yearly fee and to be fair and honest with your customers.

If you are not a member of a specialty club join now the one that fosters the bird that you breed. Don't expect a mere handful of men in each club to carry the burden of building up the pigeon industry, jump in and help. The larger the pigeon business in America grows the greater is your chance and the more profitable it will be for all concerned and by the continued good work of our specialty clubs and genuine lovers of pigeons will this industry grow.

A GENEROUS GIFT TO PIGEONDOM
Trophy Cup offered by Jack M. Pun on White Kings. Specialty clubs offer many cups and special prizes at the leading shows.

CHAPTER XXXVII

RAISING YOUNGSTERS

Very Careful Attention Must be Given—Squabs Weaned by Parents—Transferred to the Rearing Loft—Proper Feeding—Fresh Water, etc.—Working with the Youngsters—Training Them for the Show Room—Care the Youngsters Get is Bound to Reflect.

Raising youngsters to maturity is an undertaking which should be given very careful attention as they may be materially aided in their growth or given a decided set back according to the attention which they receive from their owner.

As soon as the squabs are between four and five weeks of age they are either pushed out of the nest by the parent birds or they fall out on the floor of the loft. They should be allowed to stay on the loft floor for about a week in order that they might learn, from the adult birds, how to eat from the feeders and drink from the fountains. Thus they become weaned for having reached this age the parent birds stop feeding them and they have to learn to eat.

As soon as they are weaned they are transferred to the rearing pen which is arranged just like a breeding loft. I favor having a much longer fly to this pen in order that the young birds might have more room in which to fly and thereby have more chance for development. If at all possible always separate the youngsters from the old birds for if they are kept together the old birds will be crowded, the youngsters will always be in the way and as the young birds grow older there will be incessant fighting in the pen which of course means less work and more broken eggs. As I have said before, keep unmated birds out of the breeding pens.

Having the youngsters by themselves you must keep them

bountifully supplied with sound clean grain where they can get it at any time they might wish to eat. Feed them a balanced ration so that they might derive the benefits therefrom and grow as they should. Never feed scratch grain for it does not contain the proper amount of nutriment. Do not stint youngsters in their feed.

Fresh water should be ever before them as should a plentiful supply of health grit. Do not overlook the charcoal and rock salt. Salt in this form is very essential to the growing bodies of the young birds. Be sure to keep everything in and around their loft in a sanitary condition so that disease in any form may be avoided and should it happen to show up in one of the birds remove the affected bird immediately for the others might contract the disease.

Work with your youngsters. If you see any promising birds in the lot tame them and train them for the show room. If I were asked how to condition a bird for the show room I would say "start working with it when it is growing and raise it properly, training it as it grows so that posing will be second nature. Teach them to show off to best advantage." Tame birds are very easily handled by the judges and win their admiration very quickly. Many a big winner is made right in the rearing pen. The wise breeder realizes this and starts with his show string when they are youngsters.

The care which you give your youngsters is bound to reflect later and the man who raises his young birds properly is sure to reap a reward later. Do not leave your youngsters to shift for themselves, so to speak, but watch them and nurse them into what you would have them when grown. Many a young bird is ruined by careless feeding and indifferent attention and on the other hand many a winner is made by the opposite.

CHAPTER XXXVIII

HELPFUL HINTS

Fifty Practical and Pertinent Pointers on Pigeon Breeding.

1. Pigeons have no teeth, therefore it is necessary to feed them Health Grit so they can grind their food.

2. Do not try to start where some of the leading breeders are now. Be willing to start small and learn the business as you go.

3. Lettuce leaves, cabbage leaves and Swiss chard make excellent green food for pigeons. They are also fond of green sprouted oats but only the green blades should be given to them, never the sprouted seeds.

4. Stale bread crumbs are relished by pigeons. Be sure, however, that they are not mouldy.

5: Common pigeons are the least profitable of all. It does not pay to breed them even if they fly at large.

6. Unhealthy breeding stock cannot and will not produce efficiently.

7. Keep the ground of the fly covered with clean, sharp sand. Once every month spade the ground in the fly, rake it down smooth and cover it with a good layer of sand.

8. A little discouragement proves the sticking qualities of the breeder.

9. A poor man with a determination can make as much of a success with squabs as a wealthy one.

10. Pigeon breeding requires putting good common sense into practice.

11. Do not overlook giving your birds their bath water.

12. Baths do no harm to pigeons but should be given on clear, warm days.

13. Keep your birds tame; they will work better if you do.

14. Never rush into your lofts. Always go into your lofts quietly.

15. Do not place much confidence in the man who is continually making glaring claims for his breeding stock.

16. Line breeding, if properly practiced, is the most successful way of establishing a strain.

17. If you line breed be very careful about the out-cross which some breeders use.

18. An out-cross is a cross on another strain which admits new blood into your own strain.

19. Never feed your birds on the ground. The feed is liable to become damp and sour and cause sour crop.

20. Be careful about feeding too much wheat as an excessive amount of it will cause loose bowels.

21. Never feed cracked corn if it can possibly be avoided.

22. The self-feeder system of feeding is the most modern and the most sanitary.

23. Save labor and you save money.

24. Never leave dirty water in the bath pans. It is not healthy for your birds.

25. A paralized wing is usually the result of lead poisoning. Never leave empty paint cans in your flys. If it rains in them and the birds drink the water look out for wing trouble.

26. Scald all drinking vessels once a week and scrub them until clean.

27. Should you feed twice daily, always be on hand at the feeding hour.

28. One man can easily care for one thousand pairs of pigeons if he uses system.

29. Feed salt to your pigeons only in the form of rock salt. Never feed loose salt as it will kill them.

30. Standard-bred means bred to a recognized standard.

31. A cross-bred bird is the offspring of a pair of birds in which the cock and hen were of different breeds.

32. As a rule cross-bred birds are not a success for commercial squab production.

33. Clean your lofts once every two or three weeks and sprinkle the floor with air slaked lime.

34. A good coat of whitewash once a year is a good thing for the interior of your lofts, being a good disinfectant.

35. Any time of the year is a good time for saving youngsters for breeding stock.

36. It is essential to keep your birds properly banded.

37. Remember that it takes properly balanced rations to make healthy breeding stock and permit them to produce plump squabs.

38. Don't be forever giving your birds medicine.

39. Use discretion when working with your birds.

40. If your competitor produces a better bird than you do don't get discouraged but determine to do better next time.

41. Remember that the man who argues against self-feeders is, as a rule, too narrow minded to realize the advantages of this system of feeding and in some cases too small to pay the cost of the feeders.

42. Never save skinny squabs for breeding stock for they will never develop properly.

43. Utility stock bred to a standard is the best for squab production.

44. To hold a pigeon properly place the hand around and over both wing butts. Never hold a pigeon by one wing or by a foot.

45. Pigeons cannot build nests without some sort of nesting material; this must always be kept in the lofts.

46. If a hen lays eggs that do not hatch try remating her.

47. Never keep an odd number of birds in a loft, have only mated pairs of tested workers.

48. Do not try to economize on feed. You will cut down your profits if you do this.

49. Exhibit your birds occasionally and attend the shows. You will thoroughly enjoy it all and learn a great deal by so doing.

50. Do not be without the leading pigeon magazines. You need them in order to keep abreast of the times and the pigeon press needs your support.

JACOBIN
Photo from Rosenthal Brothers, St. Louis, Mo.

CHAPTER XXXIX

FANCY BREEDS

Description of Tipplers, Pouters, Pigmy Pouters, Dragoons, Oriental Frills, Turbits, English Carriers, Barbs, Owls, Magpies, Tumblers and Helmets.

With the advent of the National Pigeon Association the breeders of this country have at last had a realization of their hopes of bringing the Utility and the Fancy into a better understanding and more friendly relation. To create a show of real

BLACK CRESTED HELMET COCK
Bred by Fairview Pigeon Lofts, Trenton, N. J.

merit and one of true educational value there must be brought together birds of both classes, thus we see the efforts of the National Pigeon Association bearing fruit for the annual show held by this organization is creating this better understanding between the Utility and the Fancy breeders and proving that both classes must be exhibited together without discrimination, in order to have a real pigeon show.

As stated in the Foreword of this book this chapter has been allotted to the Fancy breeds in order to endeavor to stimulate more interest in them not that they are not already very popular but to develop a greater interest among the breeders of the Utility in the Fancy breeds and to describe and illustrate some of these grand old breeds. It is to be regretted that time and space will not allow the writer to take up each of the Fancy

BLACK SELF TUMBLER COCK AND YOUNG BLUE BALD TUMBLER COCK
Bred by A. J. Gies, Schenectady, N. Y.

breeds and write out a descriptive standard and while only a few breeds are described there is no intention on his part of any discrimination. It is earnestly hoped that what is contained in this chapter will prove to be of much benefit to the novice who may have in mind the breeding of one of the breeds described herein.

There are numerous breeds of Fancy and Toy Pigeons. Among these we find Strassers, Larks, Nuns, Priests, Swallows, Archangels, Show Tipplers, Working Tipplers, Birmingham Rollers,

Oriental Frills, Jacobins,. English Carriers, Helmets, Russian Trumpeters, Magpies, Flights, Cumulets, English Pouters, Pigmy Pouters, Fantails, Oriental Turbits, Turbiteens, Tumblers, Tumbits, Suabians, Norwich Croppers, Frillbacks, Dragoons, Barbs, Owls, Ice Pigeons, Shields, Quakers, Starlings, Crescents and others.

The general care and management of these breeds is about the same though the breeding is different because of the wide variance in type and color. These points must be learned from

YOUNG BLUE BARRED TUMBLER HEN AND YOUNG RED SELF TUMBLER COCK
Bred by A. J. Gies, Schenectady, N. Y.

actual experience with the different birds. Most of the breeds mentioned above are bred to recognized standards and a copy of any of these standards may be had by corresponding with the proper specialty clubs.

There is one thing that will be noticed in the following breed descriptions and it is the fact that I refer to the different colored birds as varieties. This is due to the fact that my training has been to teach me to know that "Type" makes the Breed and "Color" the Variety.

TIPPLERS

In looking over a Tippler the eye of a lover of pigeons can not help but pause and admire the graceful lines of this beautiful bird. The proud head with its well proportioned and nicely set eye is very attractive indeed. The cere is small and of fine texture forming a nice circular finish around the eye. The beak is of medium length, fits snugly up into the front of the head and is dark in color. On the upper mandible

DARK BRONZE ARCHANGEL COCK
Bred by Fåirview Pigeon Lofts, Trenton, N. J.

and fitting close we find a neat wattle which is fine in texture. These points all go toward making a very attractive head on this breed.

The neck is short and tapers quickly toward the head, being stout at the shoulders. The body is short and close coupled or compact, being wedge shaped. The chest is broad, has nice depth and is carried forward having a very graceful curve from neck to keel. Against the body we find the wings carried well with strong wing butts of medium size. The flights are short and broad, overlapping each other well when stretched. Each of the primary flights are tipped with black. The tail is short and broad, carried clear of the ground and on a line with the back and is well folded.

The legs are well set under the body being short and have no feathers on shanks or toes. The feet are small, bright red in color with black toe nails.

This bird has a very erect carriage. It is a very hardy pigeon, being hard and close feathered.

The Tippler is found in four varieties, namely, the Dark Mottled, Light Mottled, Self and Chuck.

BLACK NUN COCK AND HEN
Bred by Fairview Pigeon Lofts, Trenton, N. J.

The ground color of the Dark Mottled is a rich chestnut while the markings are white. The Light Mottled have a white ground color and rich chestnut brown markings. In both varieties the distinct black bar occurs near the end of the tail and the wing primaries are tipped with a black bar.

The American Show Tippler Club is the parent association fostering this breed in America and Carl Wannemacher of Brooklyn, New York, is the Secretary.

ENGLISH POUTERS

How different from some of our Utility breeds is the grand old Pouter with his tall erect carriage and dignified appearance.

For the true fancier, who breeds his birds purely for the love of them, this breed offers most unusual opportunities.

The head of the English Pouter is small and dove shaped with straight mandibles, the upper slightly overlapping the lower one at the tip. In colors we find the beak black, horn and flesh varying with the varieties. The eyes are nicely proportioned to the size of the head and in colors are bull in whites while all other varieties have either orange or red.

"AMBASSADOR"—ENGLISH POUTER COCK
From the Browndale Strain. Bred by L. N. Smith, Minneapolis, Minn.

The neck is long and slender and carries that section which makes the breed so distinctive, namely, the globe. It is this globe which the bird inflates or puffs up like a toy-balloon. A Pouter without a good sized or well proportioned globe is not very attractive nor desired by the lovers of this breed. When this globe is inflated the bird is decidedly largest from the shoulders up for below this point it is very important that the bird be as slender and narrow as possible in girth and waist.

The breast is convex in shape while the back is narrow and tapers from the shoulders to the tail the latter also being narrow. The tail is carried well folded and held up just off the ground and on a line with the back making for the so much desired upright or erect carriage.

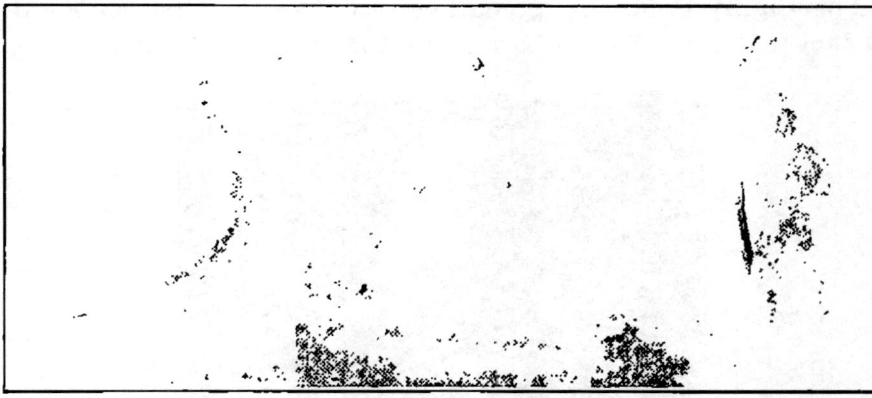

PRIZE WINNING ENGLISH CARRIERS

First bird White English Carrier cock, winner of 1st and special prize, Crystal Palace, London. Second bird, Dun English Carrier cock, winner of first prize at Crystal Palace, London. Third bird, White English Carrier hen, winner of 1st and special prize, Crystal Palace, London. —Imported by Oscar W. Opsann, New Rochelle, N. Y.

The wings are small, narrow and carried well up so as to exhibit as much of the thighs as is possible, the tips meeting on top of the tail.

The legs of the English Pouter are another very important section and the longer they are the more valuable the specimen in this respect. They should be bent at the hock or knee, slightly backwards and inwards but not too much so as to present what is known as cow-hocks. The shanks, that portion of the leg from the hock joint to the ankle should be as long as possible and very closely feathered with short white feathers in all varieties. The feet are covered with long white feathers that are known as slippers.

The standard varieties of English Pouters are Blues, Blacks, Reds, Yellow-pieds and Whites.

The National Pouter Association of America is the leading English Pouter Club in this country, of which Charles F. Wagner, 2 Toronto Street, Toronto, Canada, is Secretary.

PIGMY POUTERS

The Pigmy Pouter is a smaller bird than the English Pouter; in fact it is intended to be a miniature English Pouter in type.

DUN ENGLISH CARRIER COCK
Special Prize Winner, National Pigeon Show, Oakland, Calif., 1921.
Bred by O. B. Lindberg, Los Angeles, Calif.

This breed is a very popular one indeed and has a veritable host of admirers. It is a very graceful and proud bird.

The Pigmy has a small head in proportion to the size of the bird. The eye is well proportioned and is colored in all varieties except in the whites which have bull eyes. The cere is fine in texture. A small wattle of fine texture is desired while the beak should be made up of straight mandibles with the upper one slightly overlapping the lower. The globe is rather large and raises well up against the point of the beak. A slight fullness is shown at the back of the neck which at the front of the globe stands out very full and round.

From the globe downward the bird is very slender, the waist being very narrow, the shoulders are hollow and the back long and narrow. The breast is narrow and more or less flat. The wings are carried well up against the body with the wing butts well hidden. The tail is carried on a continuation of the line of the back and is just above the floor when the bird is standing erect. A small bird is desired, the smaller the better.

The legs of the Pigmy are long and slender and are set under the bird so that when it stands erect the ball of the foot is on a plumb line from the eye. The legs are covered with short

SILVER PIGMY POUTER COCK
Bred by Fairview Pigeon Lofts, Trenton, N. J.

soft feathers and are so covered as to allow no portion of the flesh to show, this being what is known to Pouter breeders as "stocking-legged." The feet have longer feathers that are coarser and are well spread. These feathers allow no exposure of flesh on top of the feet and are known as "slippers."

In type the bird is an erect one of long slender proportions. The carriage is therefore very proud and graceful.

The Pigmy Pouter is bred in the following well-known varieties: Pieds or Black, Blue, Red, Yellow and Silver and Plain Color or White. According to the Pigmy standard an "Any Other Color" class is allowed and is composed of Mealies, Creams,

Sandies, Chequers, Splashes and Mismarked standard-color birds.

The leading specialty clubs for this breed are the International Pigmy Pouter Association of which V. K. Butler, 530 North Charles St., Baltimore, Md., is Secretary and the Central Pigmy Pouter Club of which R. J. Nash, 2924 Woodland Ave., Kansas City, Mo., is Secretary. Both will gladly furnish further information concerning this breed.

BLACK BARB COCK
Bred by E. H. Trissler, Lancaster, Pa.

ENGLISH CARRIERS

In giving this short description of the English Carrier it is very fortunate indeed that I am able to print herewith, through the courtesy of Mr. Oscar W. Opsann of New Rochelle, N. Y., three excellent photos of specimens of this grand breed. Each of the birds shown is a first prize winner at the famous Crystal Palace (London) Show. It seems to me that our breeders of the Carrier would do well to study these photographs in connection with the official standard for the breed.

The head of the Carrier is long and narrow measuring about 2¾ inches from the tip of the beak to the back of the skull. The beak likewise is long but stout. At the junction of the head and beak we find a round wattle which should be as large as possible. There is scarcely any distinguishing line bewteen the parts of the wattle on upper and lower mandible when they are closed. This wattle is of a powdery white color. Around the eye we see an eye cere that is wide and firm in texture, not as fine as in other breeds but heavier so to speak. Here we note something a little unusual in pigeons namely that the eye cere rises slightly above the crown of the skull. In color we find the iris of the eye to be deep red in all varieties except whites which have "bull" or black eyes.

The back of the Carrier is straight and slopes from the shoulders to rump. The shoulders are flat and broad and as one looks at this bird he sees muscular power owing to these broad shoulders and protruding wing butts. The keel shows a moderate depth while the chest is wide at the front but from a side view it does not present a protruding curve. The neck is moderately long and slender and arches nicely under the beak to throat.

In feather this bird has long flights which are carried well up against the body and which rest on top of the tail. The tail feathers are long, of medium width at the tip and carried clear of the ground. The legs and claws are free from feathering. The body feathering is short and fits close making the bird have an appearance of firmness.

This bird is quite a large one in size, measuring as long as 18 to 20 inches from tip of beak to end of tail, while the back at shoulders is quite broad. To carry a body of this size we note stout, strong, legs well set under the bird while the feet are large and claws well spread.

We find four varieties recognized as standard namely, Blues, Duns, Blacks and Whites. The Blues have wing and tail bar markings of black; the Duns are of one color all over; the blacks are ebony with a green sheen; the Whites are a decided white with a lustre on breast and hackle.

The American Barb and Carrier Club is the specialty club fostering this breed, and O. W. Opsann of New Rochelle, N. Y. is the Secretary.

BARBS

In passing on the Barb we find another pleasing type of pigeons. As compared with the Carrier which was just described above we notice more compactness, broader lines, in fact

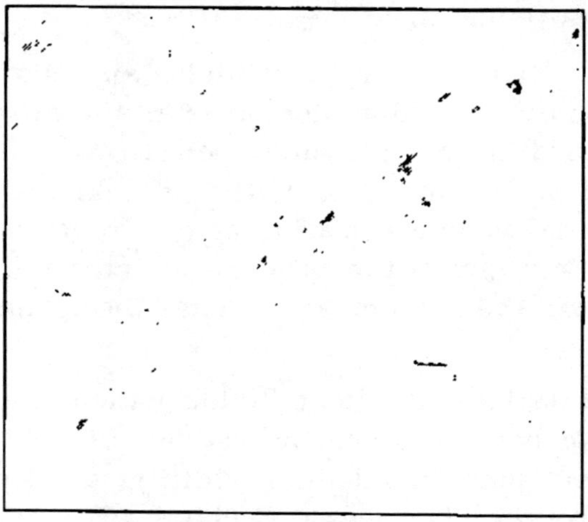

YELLOW BARB HEN
Bred by E. H. Trissler, Lancaster, Pa.

a much more "stocky" bird yet we have a medium size bird in the Barb. We have in this breed the Yellow, Black, White, Red and Light, Dark and Medium Dun varieties.

The head of the Barb is large and blocky or square and at the same time broad from front to back. The eye has a black pupil. The eye cere is a bright red in color and is circular and stands out more or less prominently. The beak is short and massive and, as the standard describes it very appropriately, of "bullfinch" shape. The mandibles are thick and of flesh color and the fine textured wattle extends nearly down to the tips of the mandibles.

The body, as said before, is short coupled having a short, stout neck blending well into wide shoulders. The breast is prominent, of good width and well rounded. In a continuation of the slope of the back we see a rather short tail. The legs are short and well proportioned.

The wing primaries or flights are long and rest on top of the tail.

The American Barb and Carrier Club is the specialty club for this breed.

OWLS

With this breed we take still another type, it being decidedly different from any of the other fancy breeds mentioned.

The head of the Owl is large and massive. It is circular in shape, in fact a full front view of the head presents a marked circle. From a side view there is an unbroken circular curve from beak to the back skull. The head is a very important section in breeding Owls as it counts more than any other section of the bird when judged by scoring. The eye is large, circular and is set practically in the center of the side of the head. In all of the colored birds the eye is currant red, except in pieds which have either bull or gravel colored eyes and whites which have either bull or claret. The eye cere is small and fine in texture. The cere is dark in blue checkers, blacks and blues, a lighter shade in all other colored birds and flesh color in whites. The beak is very short and thick and the upper mandible is a continuation of the circular forehead, from side view on its top. In color the beak is found to be black, light horn color and flesh color varying with the variety. This breed has a very small wattle that is fine in texture and powdery white in color. The Owl has a very marked gullet which fills in what would otherwise be a very hollow place at the throat.

On the front of the neck and extending well down on to the

breast there is what is known as a frill or a growth of curly feathers. This should be well developed on a good specimen. The neck is rather short; thick at the shoulders and joining them in a graceful curve all round.

The body is a very compact one with a broad, well rounded breast and a short back. The bird therefore is "cobby." To the mind of the writer it is a well proportioned bird. The tail is short and carried just clear of the floor. The wings are short and are carried well up to the body while the tips rest on the tail just in front of the tip of same. The legs are short; the feet small and toes are well spread.

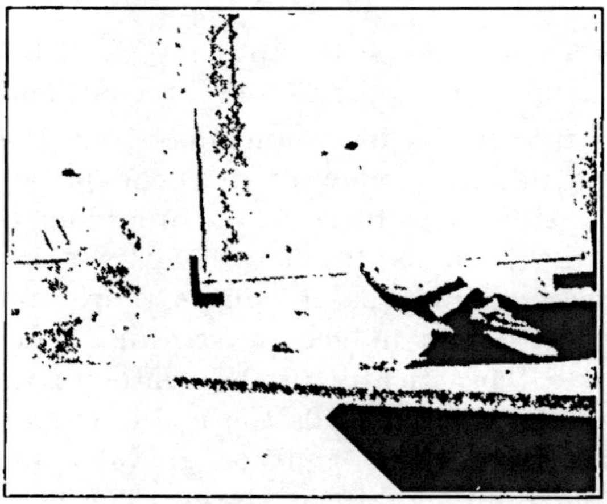

DRAGOONS
Bred by H. B. Behrens, Philadelphia, Pa.

In colors we find White, Black, Yellow, Dun, Red, Silver and Blue. These are called Standard Colors while the Standard admits of such colors as Checkers, Pieds, Mealies, Lavenders, and Silver Duns. There are three breeds of Owls, namely, English, African and Chinese or Whiskered.

The American Owl Club, which was organized in 1893, is the specialty club for this breed and L. F. Stichler of Mt. Penn, Pa., is the Secretary.

DRAGOONS

What lover of pigeons could look upon a pen of Dragoons and not admire this grand old breed? In their several colors these birds of medium size are most attractive. We find the breed in the following varieties: Blues, Blue Chequers, Grizzles, Red Chequers, Mealies, Blacks, Silvers, Reds, Yellows and White.

The head of the Dragoon is wedge-shaped and broad and has a gradual curve from the beak to the back of the skull. The wattle is fairly large and is described in the standard as "Peg"

MR. BEHRENS AND A FEW OF HIS DRAGOONS

shaped, a very good description indeed. The mandibles are stout and straight and should show as little wattle as possible on the lower one,—how different from the wattle of the Carrier this section is. The color of the beak varies with the varieties of the breed, there being three beak colors namely, horn color, black and flesh color. The cere is small, firm and circular. Like the beak the color of the cere varies with the varieties and we find damson and flesh color. The eye is prominent and we have in this breed ruby, bull, and red iris.

The breast is broad and well rounded. The back is broad and sweeps off toward the tail narrowing from shoulders to the rump. The tail is in a continuation of the line of the back yet carried clear of the ground. The wings are well developed and as the shoulders are quite broad there is a sign of muscular power. The wing butts should not stand out from the body at front. Flights rest on top of the tail. The neck is of medium length. Legs are of good size and well set under the body.

The American Dragoon Club is the specialty club for this breed of which H. B. Behrens of Philadelphia is Secretary.

TURBITS

For many years the writer has been a very great admirer of Turbits and sometimes I wonder why I have never bred them. These little birds are very attractive and have a great many admirers at every show.

The head of the Turbit is large and broad with a high and prominent forehead. The cheeks are well bulged giving a "down-faced" appearance. The beak is short and thick, the upper mandible being a continuation of the curvature of the forehead as seen from side view. The wattle is small and fits close so as not to break the curvature of the forehead when viewed from the side and is fine in texture. The eyes are large and prominent and are encircled by pale flesh colored eye-ceres which are fine in texture. The eyes are bull. The Turbit shows much gullet.

The neck is moderately short and broad forming nice smooth curves where it joins the shoulders and breast. The body proper is small and compact and very dignified or upright. The breast is full, round and carried well up. The wings are short and carried close up to the body. The tail is short and carried well up above the floor. The flights rest on top of the tail. The legs are short and free from feathering on shanks and toes, while but little of the thigh shows. The color of the legs is bright red. On the back of the neck we find what is known as a mane which is, as the standard describes it, knife-like and

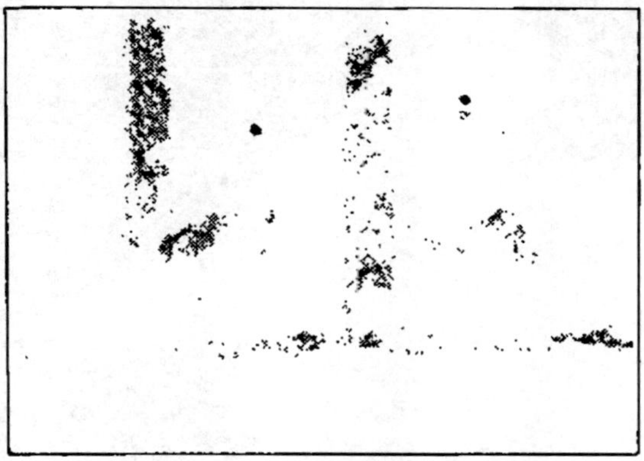

A PAIR OF BLUE TURBITS
Bred by Rosenthal Brothers, St. Louis, Mo.

begins well down on the shoulders and going upward terminates at and above the back skull in what is known as the peak. On the throat beginning at the gullet and extending well down on to the breast we find a frill.

The ground color of Turbits is white with colored wings and in all cases we find each variety having ten white primaries. The varieties are Black, Blue, Red, Yellow, Dun and Silver.

The American Turbit Club is the specialty club for this breed and E. B. Ulrich of Reading, Pa., is the Secretary.

ORIENTAL FRILLS

Among the most popular of the Fancy breeds we find the Oriental Frills standing out very prominently. They are very attractive and make ideal exhibition birds which no doubt accounts for their great popularity.

ORIENTAL FRILL
Bred by John Buscher, St. Louis, Mo.

The head is large and round, being formed in a continuous curve from the back skull to the beak and from eye to eye with no indentations or flatness in this section. The cheeks are full and well rounded. The eyes are large and prominent while the cere is small of fine texture and of a pale flesh color. The beak is short, fits closely and like that of the Turbit it forms an unbroken continuation of the curvature of the forehead as viewed from the side. A wattle of medium size and fine texture is noted in these birds. A crest or peak is found at the back of the head just above the skull and from this springs a mane which extends well down between the shoulders.

The neck should be of great length, broad at junction with body proper and well arched showing good thickness. The gullet starts at the frill and extends to a point near the tip of the lower mandible and is full. The frill is well developed and covers the breast nicely. The intersection of gullet and beak

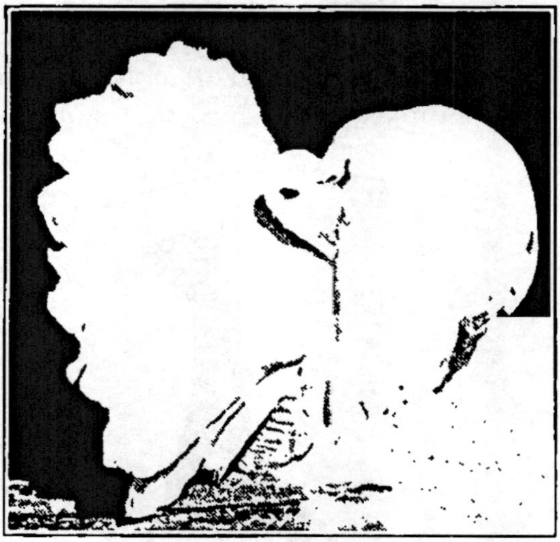

WHITE FANTAIL COCK

First at Chicago Pigeon Show, December 1920. Bred and owned by Kelly and Altpeter, Milwaukee, Wis.

should find the latter presenting more or less of a "down-faced" appearance. The breast is well developed, of nice proportion being full, round and prominent. The back and body taper off toward the tail, the latter being of moderate length. The wings are also of medium length.

The legs are covered with feathers down to the toe nails, being of moderate length and well set under the bird.

The Frill is a dignified and active bird being very erect and graceful in carriage.

The foregoing description fits the several varieties named

in the official standard for Oriental Frills, these varieties being, Satinettes, Blondinettes, Bluettes, Silverettes, Vizor, Turbiteen, Oriental Turbit and Domino, however in the last two varieties the legs are free from feathering. The specialty club for these birds is the American Oriental Frill Club of which I. B. Brennaman of Lebanon, Pennsylvania, is Secretary.

MAGPIES

In the Magpie we find a wonderful exhibition bird and one that is very popular indeed. The bird is a small one, the cocks

PHOTO FROM PAINTING OF IDEAL MAGPIE
Courtesy of D. J. Ogilvie, Long Island, N. Y.

weighing $9\frac{1}{2}$ to $10\frac{1}{2}$ ounces and hens from $8\frac{1}{2}$ to $9\frac{1}{2}$ ounces. The accompanying cut is from a photograph of an oil painting of the Ideal Magpie as recognized by the Magpie Club.

The head of the Magpie is long and thin with a round skull and long narrow face which tapers into a long thin beak, the latter being straight and fine. The eye is white or pearl color with a black pupil. The eye cere is small and fine in texture. In color the eye cere varies from a white tint to a coral red. There is a small wattle of fine texture. The neck is long and thin and shows no gullet or fullness at throat, the thinnest section of the neck being just below the head and gently swelling towards the shoulders.

ENGLISH SHOW HOMER, "KING EDWARD"
Owned by C. R. King, Hayward, Calif.

The body is long, slender and round, gracefully tapering from front to rear. The chest is full and round but not broad. Legs are rather long and straight showing no tendency to being knock kneed or cow hocked. The legs and feet from hock joint down are free from feathers. The tail is rather long and is in a line with the back being carried just clear of the ground. The flights are carried well folded up to the side of the body with the tips resting on the tail. The plumage is close but is not hard feathered.

In coloring the Magpie has the color on the head, neck, breast, back, saddle, and tail and the remainder of the feathering is pure white as shown in the accompanying cut. The colors are deep and lustrous.

The several varieties are Blacks, Yellows, Reds, Blues, Silvers, and Duns. The Blues and Silvers have black tail bars.

IDEAL MOOREHEAD TUMBLER

CHAPTER XL

COMMON PIGEONS

Why Common Pigeons are not Profitable.

On several occasions the writer has been asked if it would not be just as profitable to breed common pigeons and allow them to fly at large as it would be to house up an equal number of pure bred birds. On the face of the matter the experienced breeder realizes the folly of attempting to make money out of common pigeons. It cannot be done scccessfully. As a parallel case we never see poultrymen endeavoring to breed common chickens or mongrels for egg production or market purposes. The answer is plain enough. The breeding is not in the bird's make-up and it is therefore not capable of producing proper results.

The common pigeon is a mongrel with the blood of several breeds flowing in its veins. They mate up promiscuously according to their own likes and dislikes and cannot therefore be relied upon to produce anything of value. These birds fly at large in the majority of cases and live in the eaves of houses rearing their squabs in the best manner possible. For a living they pick up whatever they can find on the ground and streets. It is not bred in them to produce plump white skinned squabs of marketable value.

When we confine a bunch of these birds and care for them as we would for pure bred stock we soon find out the folly of it all. The speed of breeding is lacking and any breeder would be extremely lucky to average six pairs per year for his flock of mongrels and what squabs he did get would be a conglomerate bunch of skinny, dark skinned birds fit only for feeding his dogs on. This has been my experience for I have both tried it myself and have seen others make this test.

Some believe in the grade proposition—that is they cross pure bred cocks with mongrel hens and vice versa. This will do some good at least—it always does as may be seen in grade cattle and grade poultry yet the writer could never see the logic of it at all. My reason for this statement is that at best this is not a half blood proposition because there is always, almost without exception, the blood of the third breed in the offspring and it is therefore a mongrel. Why waste full bred blood lines in mixing stock because the results obtained are never as satis-

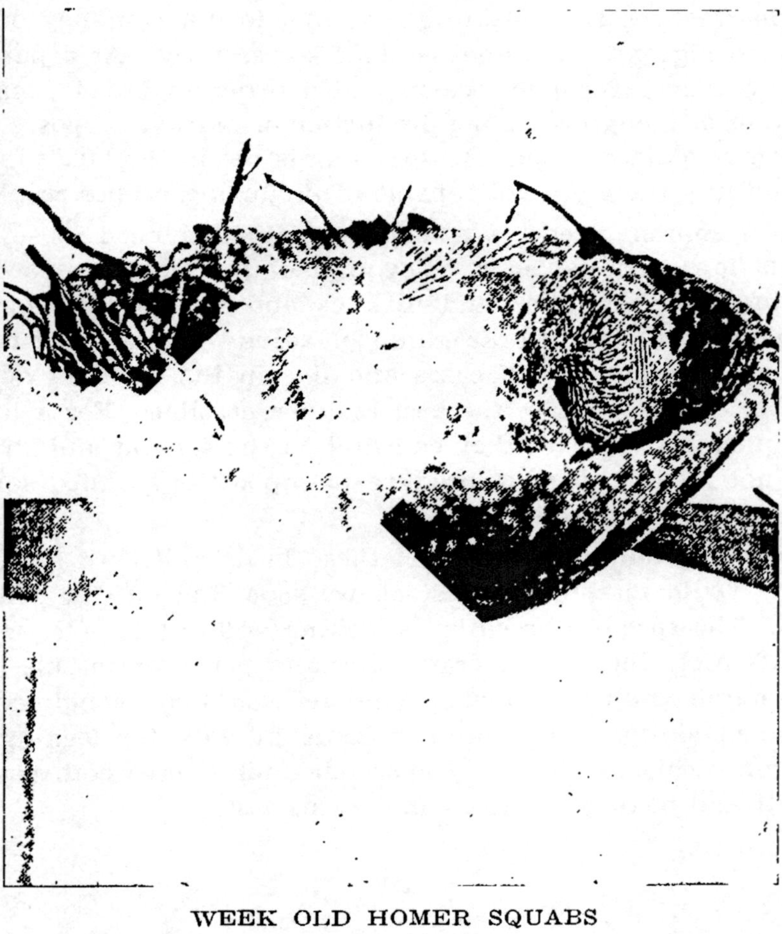

WEEK OLD HOMER SQUABS

factory as if the pure bred blood had been mated up within itself and kept intact as such. It is far better, in my opinion, to have three or four pairs of pure bred birds than twenty pairs of crosses which are made up of common pigeon blood and that of the pure breeds.

The novice could make no greater mistake than to attempt to breed common pigeons, either under wire or by allowing them to fly at large. He will meet with terrible disappointment if he does so.

INDEX

ADVERTISEMENTS

MEMORANDA

MEMORANDA

MEMORANDA

MEMORANDA

MEMORANDA

MEMORANDA

MEMORANDA

Lightning Source UK Ltd.
Milton Keynes UK
UKOW05f2025270913

218077UK00003B/39/P